PS2124.C3
The novels of Henry James; a study.

3 9367 03293784 7

COLLEGE OF SAN MATEO LIBRARY

D1735991

The Novels of
Henry James

COPYRIGHT, 1905, BY ALICE BOUGHTON

Henry James

From a photograph by Alice Boughton

The Novels of
Henry James

A Study

By

Elisabeth Luther Cary

With a Bibliography by
Frederick A. King

HASKELL HOUSE
Publishers of Scholarly Books
NEW YORK
1964

First published in 1905

HASKELL HOUSE

Library of Congress Catalog Card Number: 65-15897

Haskell House Catalogue Item # 520

PRINTED IN UNITED STATES OF AMERICA
65287

CONTENTS

CHAPTER	PAGE
Introductory Chapter	1
I.—American Character	20
II.—The Genius of Place	95
III.—The Question of Wealth	119
IV.—Imagination	144
V.—Philosophy	169
Bibliography	189

The Novels of Henry James
A Study

Introductory Chapter

AFTER the work of an important writer has extended over more than a quarter of a century, he becomes, properly enough, a subject, if not for final critical judgment, at least for something more than cursory consideration. It is time to think of him not as the author of independent works, each pleasing or displeasing to a sufficiently various public, but as the creator through his accumulated accomplishment of an impression both definite and general. It is inconceivable that the little world of readers and thinkers to which he addresses himself is in precisely the same temper of mind as if he had not lived and written. He has either enriched or impoverished it. He has either raised or lowered its opinion of the human nature so long discussed by him. He has either quickened or dulled its vision for beauty in character, art, and the external world. Above all, he has inevitably made more clear the elusive boundaries of what is worth while in a life of multitudinous choice. He has emphasised by a thousand minute accents, if not by obvious broad strokes, his preoccupations in the domain of morals. In a word, he has become an influence to be prized or to be deprecated, he has become a part of the mental climate to which we owe so many of our joys and afflictions. He belongs indefeasably to our consciousness and can never be separated from our memories. In the case of a living writer we frequently ignore this intimate relation with the public. It is natural to take it for granted, much as we take for granted the bonds of family, so difficult is it to estimate at its true value to us the note of a voice still speaking for our warning, our instruction, our amusement, or our comfort.

The voice of Mr. Henry James is one to which we have long been accustomed. For something more than thirty years it has sounded in harmony with our finer æsthetic predilections. None who heard it in the early time, when the trip to Europe was not yet a common yearly satisfaction for even the "cultivated minority," when the foreign galleries were not yet filled with American tourists, can forget its irresistible note of youthful receptivity, of eloquent rejoicing in "the beautiful scenic properties of English life," of bright suggestion that only a "poor disinherited Yankee" could properly appreciate the "points" of admirable England. As it grew more and more apparent that this England was to retain its fascination in the eyes of the itinerant critic, and that his interest in the enchanting English landscape was to wrap itself closely about the figures with which, he early noted, an English landscape is always amply relieved, it became a matter almost of anxiety to discover in what frame of mind he was to interrogate the much entangled human scene on which his eyes were so

HENRY JAMES'S HOUSE AT RYE, SUSSEX.
Etched by Mr. Lionel Lindsay.

intelligently bent. Already seen to be gifted with an extraordinary capacity for self-expression, and amazingly perceptive, responsive, accurate, and imaginative, he set us at liberty to indulge in brilliant expectations. His early novels seemed the vanguard of a body of literature that should win an easy triumph over the commonplace. Some of us shook our heads, to be sure, over what we vaguely suspected to be their "foreign flavour," their apparent derivation from sources with which we were not ourselves intimately acquainted; but there was compensation in having the pleasure of such an undeniably rare quality, and furnished for us by one of our own race, of our national family. He has told us that to be at once fresh and ripe of mind was what Lowell predominantly understood by being a good American, and on his own part he has never ceased to be one in that particular sense.

But if it is true that "America is Opportunity," it was logical enough to feel, as many early readers of Mr. James vociferously did feel, that a species of practical joke was cruelly played upon that innocent country when its most promising and competent novelist made prompt use of the opportunity to leave it. It was at least, perhaps, a measure of the American desire to possess him that his flitting was so openly resented. Such naïve resentments have slipped, however, into the background of the national consciousness. Concern for the dignity of the country has come with time to mean in serious minds something very different from this immature sentiment of provincial pride. What the "good American" now thinks about with perhaps less optimism than formerly, but surely with a finer ardour, is how his country may avoid the choice commemorated in Emerson's significant poem, how it may learn clearly to distinguish diadems from fagots and firmly to grasp the better gifts of the hypocritic days in manners, in morals, and in learning, as well as in commerce and mechanical science. He finds it not merely agreeable but quite essential to his peace of mind to enlarge so far as he can his horizon, to listen to cosmopolitan voices from the more ancient civilised centres of the world. He finds it good not only to

——hear the deeds of kings,
Which were fools and which were wise.

but to hear also of societies older than our own with their fixed and mellowed forms, to reflect upon the types produced by them, and the types impossible for them to produce.

From this point of view the patriot must inevitably welcome, almost with a sense of pious gratitude, a long series of impressions made upon a mind prepared to receive the fine, elusive, imperceptible seed of English and European influences, to nourish it with the substance of a rich intelligence, and bring it to a luxuriant fruitage of ripe reflection. Perhaps it is indeed necessary to belong to the disinherited in order to look on at the overwhelming complicated social spectacle of London with a gaze at once interested and detached, to separate from its brilliant confusion the elements of similarity and contrast so indispensable to the student of comparative sociology in the untechnical and practically unlimited sense of a phrase curiously restricted and perverted in the modern vocabulary. The novelist of manners, to use again a phrase commonly limited to only half its meaning, is of necessity a person dedicated to his occupation. If the wisdom of a learnèd man cometh by opportunity of leisure, the wise records of a leisure class require nevertheless an immense amount of labour. It is, perhaps, as the diligent recorder of a leisure class, with its intricately combined and differentiated characteristics, that Mr. James most appeals to readers eager for the fullest possible data of human society. Along this line he has laboured for us of the present generation as no one else has laboured, and has fixed with exquisite analysis types and conditions that are already ceasing to exist in life and are nowhere else than in his novels adequately commemorated. Even when we find ourselves in special instances critical of his choice and in doubt concerning its sustained significance, we are obliged to admit that he alone of the present time has undertaken to produce for us a picture of international social relations, drawn in the presence of the model, and with a patience and authority inspired by an infinitely serious purpose. His cumulative statement of his impressions has the dignity of mature, considered, highly developed art. It is the synthesis of deliberately acquired knowledge, and bears none of the marks of hasty seeing or superficial learning. In using the simile of the painter's art to express his performance, we are more than usually justified, for his method is closely akin to that of the painter if we make due allowance for the greater flexibility of his medium. He reproduces appearances with sufficient regard to selection, representing in his work the seen and recording the fact that certain things are unseen. From these appearances we may judge what the reality is; from these beautifully rendered effects we may infer causes; but what is not left for inference, what is impressed upon us so forcibly as to admit of no contradiction, is the sincerity of the artist and the consequent importance as matter for consideration of his art. He has many times been said to resemble the French in his methods, and he himself has acknowledged a special allegiance to the essentially Gallic spirit of Balzac. But the quality in which we can see most clearly such a resemblance, the quality of conscientiousness, is stronger with him and deeper than with any Frenchman known to modern letters. So far as he displays that admirable virtue in the matter—the mere matter, it is tempting for an English writer to say,—of his technique he is certainly closely allied to the French mind which works toward "style" with an indifference to the labour involved, a love not merely of the end but of the means to such an end, unknown to any other race. But conscientiousness in its deeper and subtler sense, the French, it has been noted by a critic himself at once deep and subtle, conspicuously lack. Mr. James, on the other hand, has carried it into regions which it illumines with an extraordinary light. It has become increasingly true of him that he reaches depths and crannies of character and temperament to which none of his predecessors could have penetrated, making his way through the baffling layers of cant and custom and back of the sturdy file of obvious motives guarding the secrets of our innermost being, by means of a passion for truth too intense and moving to be classified as philosophy. It has been said indeed that Mr. James has no philosophy, but it cannot be denied that he has a religion in the general and large meaning of the word. In the domain of his art it is his religion to reveal not perhaps so much as may be possible of life, but life as close as possible to its source, life as little as possible concealed by its mask or observed at second hand. Reviewing his work from the tentative charming experiments, confessions, and blithe confidences of his wandering years to *The Golden Bowl,* with its close texture like old rich hand-woven tapestry, the tendency of his effort, preconceived, we may imagine, and consistently held, is sufficiently apparent. It is nothing, surely, but this, or at all events nothing less than this: to come by incorrigible patience and unwearying perception at the life of the soul, and to render this with an art worthy of the difficult, the well-nigh impossible subject. Something of the sort he has, indeed, said, impersonally, in his essay on Pierre Loti, which, like all his essays, contains wide suggestion for the fascinated student of his point of view. The soul, he suggests, may appear to the moralising observer "a romantic, moonlighted landscape, with woods and mountains and dim distances, visited by strange winds and murmurs." It is thus, certainly, that it appears to him, and if in his thickly peopled life he has lacked, and in his writings has somewhat shown the lack, of frequent communion with the good brown earth in places not yet humanised by the presence of man, he has made of the dim underworld in which ideas and emotions are born a place of infinite loneliness and romance. These inner scenes upon which he looks are as filled with the unfamiliar and the inaccessible as the island of Crusoe's fame or the New World appearing to the first explorer of the Western hemisphere. This interrogation of the invisible united to an unremitting effort toward completeness of evocation constitutes his extraordinary distinction. It places him as he appears in his later novels, quite apart not only in accomplishment, but, one might positively say, in aim from all other novelists living or dead. Great as Thackeray was, greater in a certain clear control over his material than any one of his century, he nevertheless was contented with the obvious, and in this contentment unquestionably lies much of the secret not of his genius, but of his popularity. George Meredith, to whom the human spirit, and even more particularly the human mind, is the most interesting subject in the world, declines to provide for it a credible social environment. Against a group of modern French novelists Mr. James himself brings the charge of neglect for "the multitudinous, adventurous experience of the senses," of "the deeper, stranger, subtler inward life, the wonderful adventures of the soul," and notes the apparent inability of the French imagination when it does take account of ideas and moral states, to use the same skill that is so much at its service in expressing the visible. Of Flaubert he says: "He should at least have listened at the chamber of the soul. This would have floated him on a deeper tide; above all, it would have calmed his nerves." Such expressions are of the greatest value to the critic or commentator attempting to find precisely the generalisation that will represent to the general but ungeneralising public the special combination of qualities in which abides the pre-eminence of Mr. James as a writer of fiction. If there is no egoistic satisfaction to be had from a clue so unmistakable, there is the equal, if not superior, satisfaction of having one's analysis so clearly and simply done for one. The pure consistency of his attitude is what makes Mr. James for any critic the most certain of quantities, the least really bewildering, though far from the least intricate, of problems so far as the larger aspiration and the visible goal of his labour are concerned. What he personally stands for in his criticisms, and what he indefatigably acts upon in his novels and stories, most of all in his shorter stories, is this simple and supreme idea of combining what a critic of painting would call tactile values with the greatest possible amount of spiritual truth. In other words, his technical curiosity, his ability to represent life pictorially by a multiplicity of fine observations, runs hand in hand with a curiosity far more unusual and far more difficult to satisfy, a curiosity as to moral states and responsible affections. To say this is only to say what is obvious to every interested reader of his work, but it is the natural point to start from in any co-ordinated comment on his various achievement.

I

IF we discover in work of ripe years a conspicuous value, we instinctively ask under what conditions the stream of artistic energy began to flow, where it took its rise, through what landscape, bleak or smiling, it made its way, how promptly or gradually it enlarged its borders and extended its sweep, if it were clear at its source or turbid, slow or impetuous in its movement. In many cases the thoughts of youth are far from long thoughts; what seems profoundly important to the pride and passion of young minds becomes definitely unimportant to the calmer mood of middle age. Especially the impulse toward intellectual labour is curiously apt to wane. The idleness of the young is negligible compared to the idleness of the middle years, the deadly peace that follows a certain amount of successful striving and that marks the end of true accomplishment. When, then, we are rejoiced by the vision of a noble fruitful activity, which after nearly forty years of work in the most exacting and exhausting field of literature permits no perfunctoriness, no superficiality or indifference, we are keen to trace the inspiration to its beginnings and search where it is least tortuous, least complicated by the contributory streams of experience, for its original quality. The early works of a writer who has proven himself of lasting fibre are more than merely the charming and touching efforts of fragile immaturity to meet the great mocking initiated world on equal terms: they are frequently the key to his larger intention; they show with what his mind has been primarily occupied, before the many-coloured complexities of his journey through life have come into question. If he has finally achieved the effect of unity in his later work, compounded of ten thousand observations and reflections on the human scene, it is curiously interesting to see the earlier unity formed with only a few predilections and a handful of data.

If, especially, a writer has made himself a recorder and interpreter of society on any extended scale, if he has depicted the life of gregarious people, and has reproduced in multitudinous figures the manners, opinions, ideas, and temper of the social world of his prolonged study, it is rewarding to look back to his attitude toward the narrower social world of his early experience, to observe how he laid the foundations of intimate knowledge necessary to his purpose, and whether his interest in civilisation struck at first the provincial local note or betrayed an appreciation of wide horizons. As Mr. James is an American and has chosen for his most frequently recurring theme the attitude in which America and England stand toward each other on the social field, every shade of expression noted by him in the two fair faces thus confronting one another with mingled bewilderment, friendliness, and antagonism, has its special value. If thirty years ago his observation was less practised and instructed than now, it was not less refined and thorough. And certainly we cannot fully enjoy the splendid various subjects of his art as his steady hand guides and governs it without spending a little time with it as an integral performance, an organic whole developed as is the way of life from simplicity toward complexity, from the homogeneous toward the heterogeneous, not losing the vital essence by which alone it is interesting and human. Any notice, then, of the novels of Mr. James that fails to take account of the very earliest, of *Watch and Ward* and *Roderick Hudson* and *The Europeans*, as a part of the pattern in the dense rich web to which belong *The Ambassadors* and *The Golden Bowl*, misses, one might say, the fun of criticism; misses at all events the merry game of finding in the earlier work the cross references and completions and extensions of the later, of finding in the later the suggestions and sympathies and explanations of the earlier, of bringing them all together in the mind to form a broad and definite impression more satisfying, we are free to hope, than a fragmentary and desultory discussion of even the most important parts could yield.

Mr. James almost may be said to have begun work before the end of his first decade. At all events, he has given us a charming and revealing picture of an early childhood largely spent in poring over the numbers of *Punch*, through the illustrations of which he became familiar with the units of the vast London throng, with the cabmen and costermongers, the little pages in buttons, the gentlemen of the hunt and the Row, the small boys in tall hats and Eton jackets, the pretty girls in striped petticoats and mushroom-shaped coiffures. He was already consciously engaging in that preparation for the trans-Atlantic adventure which has formed the text of so many of his later stories. He knew the names of the London streets, he tells us, of the theatres, and of many of the shops; he knew what to expect from Kensington Gardens and Piccadilly, he knew the very aspect of a Westminster slum. He was collecting his baggage betimes, arranging it in portable form, and with such competence that, when at the age of twelve he finally set forth upon the travels that even then seemed to him to have been perpetually postponed, he was ready to take his place at once on deck, scanning the new horizon with a gaze no less youthfully eager for its precocious initiation. We may very well imagine that to the eyes of the child it was a natural substitution of the great pictorial world for the limited but largely suggesting picture - book. And the lovers of picture-books and of an art of illustration that has fallen into a trance of the most alarming character, if it be not actually dead, may delight to fall upon the description—it occurs in an essay on George Du Maurier—of the effect upon a susceptible adolescent mind of the rich and life - communicating line of John Leech. That the famous illustrator assisted in the forming of this childish vision of an elaborate civilisation is an agreeable fragment of information for us, hinting how great talents have always served each other, how masters in one art and another have played into each other's hands, how many hundreds of such influences have been assimilated in the making of a masterpiece.

It was in 1855 that the young traveller was given his opportunity to register the London of *Punch* with the immense real town. He found to his abundant joy that the impression and the reality coincided with precision, that the deep, brilliant colours of the actual scene filled the prefigured outline as though placed by the accurate hand of some old Japanese printmaker of superior skill, and thus the first note was struck for him of the gratitude which he has always so freely expressed toward those who have felt, have analysed and represented life. The London passion survived with him, renewed itself in later years, and flowered richly in his work. It was a full generation after the first visit that he paid his special tribute to the British capital as "the particular spot in the world which communicates the greatest sense of life," and it is not unimportant that he added, "a sense of the life of people of our incomparable English speech," and lingered on the kindness he felt for the London railway stations as places where one thinks

> how great we all are together in the light of heaven and the face of the rest of the world, with the bond of our glorious tongue in which we labour to write articles and books for each other's candid perusal, how great we all are, and how great is the great city

which we may unite fraternally to regard as the capital of our race.

The London passion, specific and explicit as it is with him, is, after all, the form, the mould into which is poured his richer passion for the race to which he belongs. If he vibrates with the historic sense it is not in the mood of the scholar—as the scholar oftenest defines himself to us by his works—it is in the mood of the rare individual to whom history means continuity of experience, who, wrapped in the mantle of inherited traditions and manners of thought, surveys the present also in its historic aspect, marks in it what has changed and what will change; sees the much that is fluid, the little that is fixed, in what so lightly passes under the name of "our civilisation." This faculty for seeing contrasts and evolutions, for living on the one hand with sensibilities in full reaction to the impressions of the tremendous carnival of modern society, and on the other hand with affections clustering and clinging about the old, the dim, the ghostly, in relics of the past, this mingling of curiosity and reverence, constitutes an advantage for the recorder of manners hardly to be over-estimated. In a quite recent book, *The Awkward Age*, the step from the manners of the near past to those of the immediate present within a certain small circle of the tangential social rings making up the great capital, is taken in a way to indicate to the interested reader the constant method of the writer, a habit that seems unintermitting with him, of using the vanished scene as a touchstone for the one before us, of holding up his brilliant picture against the soft, thick background of accumulated associations to try the value of its modern tone.

For this method, however, the preparation is necessarily vast. Indefatigable interrogation of the living model, complete saturation in the composite air of reminiscent experience, without these there can be no fusion of impressions, no "atmosphere" in the sense given to the word by the painters; and it was the good fortune of Mr. James to be able to commence his studies in the one right way for achieving his result.

He was abroad until 1859, and then came back for a single decade of purely American life before he again packed his still slender and portable outfit for the return to England that was to separate him conclusively from his native country. This decade, more or less unconsciously dedicated, no doubt, to the observation of American customs and character, was to have upon his later work an effect peculiarly interesting to the American critic. It is easy to exaggerate the effect, and the safer course might be to ignore it, to assume that the later work would have been substantially the same without the brief period of study in the Harvard law-school, of escape on dusky winter afternoons into the glow of Mr. Lowell's "learned lamplight," of looking out upon beaten snow and wooden houses and lonely roads, of looking in upon crowding imaginations of motley foreign splendours, of southern colour, of Italy and England and bright, logical France. But the safer course in some instances frankly declines to be possible, and no deeply enlisted reader of the novels of Mr. James can forget that early background, that familiarity with the cool, clear New England life, to which his mature fancy repeatedly returns, whimsically, critically, with detachment, but with how much also of appreciation and understanding.

As early as 1865 he began to contribute stories to the *Atlantic Monthly*, and naturally these had in more than one case the war background. They were not very remarkable, nor did they possess many of the special qualities of the later work. In only one instance, that of the story entitled *Gabrielle de Bergerac*, in which the American note is not struck, do we get a hint of the free and gracious manner so soon to be acquired. Yet they have a present interest, since it is easy to detect in them a theory not altogether dissociated from the convictions ruling *The Sacred Fount* and *The Golden Bowl*. A search for motives of action, a freedom from sentimentality, and a marked respect for accuracy of observation are there, and if it is not yet the art that conceals art, art nevertheless is present, lending her lovely aspect to the timid interpretations of an inexperienced hand.

An article, moreover, on George Eliot in the *Atlantic* for October, 1866, sets forth certain principles of the novelist's craft already definitely conceived and firmly stated. Challenging the anti-climax in *Adam Bede*, the young author suggests that it might very well have been left to the reader to deduce from Adam's character, temperament, and state of mind his ultimate marriage with Dinah.

In every novel [he observes] the work is divided between the writer and the reader, but the writer makes the reader very much as he makes his characters. When he makes him ill, that is, makes him indifferent, he does no work, the writer does all. When he makes him well, that is, makes him interested, then the reader does quite half the labour. In making such a deduction as I have just indicated [that of Adam's probable marriage], the reader would be doing but his share of the task; the grand point is to get him to make it. I hold that there is a way. It is perhaps a secret, but until it is found out, I think that the art of storytelling cannot be said to have approached perfection.

This artistic requirement which he was not to forget is evolved with genuine penetration, and other points chosen for emphasis prove that already he had thought about what kind of a novelist he intended to make of himself, and that his struggle with his difficult medium was to be systematic. It would hardly be fair to quote extensively from the clever little article, rich as it is in suggestion, or to infer from it an inflexible plan. The harness a young man of three and twenty makes for his genius is seldom stout enough to hold any but the tamest spirit for an extended term of years. We may, however, give ourselves the satisfaction—a rare one—of perceiving at the outset that there was a plan well-cogitated and serious and we may, perhaps, extract one more passage for the fulness of its significance:

They [the novels of George Eliot] offer a completeness, a rich density of detail, which could be the fruit only of a long term of conscious contact—such as would make it much more difficult for the author to fall into the perversion and suppression of facts than to set them down literally.

An acute critic might fairly have predicted at this time that a rich density of detail would one day characterise the work of Mr. James himself, and also that it would be the fruit of nothing less than conscious contact with a world of multitudinous appearances by a mind that found it more difficult to be perversive than truthful. The secret hidden from the critical eye was the special field of his labour. In England, novels of various kinds were swarming. After a hundred years of as much struggle, error, compromise, and triumph over adverse conditions as ever went to the founding of a nation, the novel had made its place as an art and as a record of life. It was the high tide of what might be called its legitimate popularity, a popularity, that is, involving the intelligent consideration of serious minds. Thackeray had died leaving his Becky, his Blanche Amory, his Ethel Newcome, and his Beatrix to the prolonged and energetic discussion of his critics. Dickens had etched all the *figures variées* of his large queer London plate, with its rich brutality of line, its coarse discriminations, its inestimable pictorial value. Anthony Trollope had just finished *The Last Chronicles of Barset*, and with it had closed the door on his masterpieces. George Eliot had published her three great books and Meredith had written *Richard Feverel* and *Rhoda Fleming*. Even Thomas

Hardy had already appeared on the horizon with his *Desperate Remedies*. Nearly twenty years before, Balzac, in France, had been cut down by the fury of his industry. It was a world, certainly, in which a young novelist with a plan needed to keep all his wits about him to hold to his individual path: to be a student yet not bound to a master; to be plastic, susceptible, teachable and yet definite, sincere, and persistent; to cherish his freshness and bloom and avoid remaining unsophisticated and unintelligent. When *Watch and Ward* appeared in the *Atlantic*, in 1871 as the serial for the year, it offered no positive promise that such a feat was within its author's range. It was neither imitative nor strikingly original. It was a pleasant little story, not without touches of melodrama, dealing with the predicament of a young girl, whose guardian is in love with her. The fact that she owes to him her salvation from a life of destitution constitutes, however, a situation not entirely unworthy of the author of *The Wings of a Dove*. No one has ever more justly drawn the relations of obligation and gratitude, and in his first extended novel his future mastery in this difficult line at least is foreshadowed. The figures of Roger and Nora, despite their primness of outline, have thoroughly the aspect of life by virtue of their deep, their infrangible and incorruptible delicacy. The conditions weighing upon them were not common, but their interest depended on the complete lack of vulgarity in the chief actors of the crude little drama. Character as brought out by the plot was the essential matter, and thus at the very beginning the genuine note of the author's individuality was struck.

Watch and Ward was followed by a group of short stories, some of which have been republished, and others of which lie deeply buried in the early numbers of the extinct *Galaxy*. They are admirable performances, real and human in feeling, most of them touched with such tragedy as lies in the situation of sensitive temperaments and talents placed at the mercy of events. They show a spirited interest in psychological problems, with which they deal at the same time quite naturally and without the forced or pedantic suggestion from which professed students of psychology seem to find it so difficult to escape. A strong sense of the mystery of the human mind is brought home to us by such a story as *The Last of the Valerii* or *Madame de Mauves*, but it is tempered and lightened by the fascinating background of the visible world against which the most lurid accidents are set. We may read positively with a feeling of tranquillity a story of even the darkest crime if on every page we are detained and soothed by such pictures as that of Oxford in *The Passionate Pilgrim*, or that of the quiet old church of San Miniato in *The Madonna of the Future*. The human creature is, naturally, not so finely indicated. We receive an impression of much intensity of mind and heart, of a haunting curiosity concerning the supernatural, of remarkably significant dialogue; and from time to time we are face to face with a figure as successfully executed as it is ingeniously conceived—such a figure as Eugene Pickering or Longmore in *Madame de Mauves* —but in general the extreme care with which the persons of the drama are constructed is not yet sufficiently hidden; they are rather barely and austerely before us with the somewhat gaunt lines of their physiognomy well in view. They are like the first studies of a painter more intent upon mastering his instrument and reproducing with accuracy the object before him than upon attaining immediately a handsome picture for the applause of an undiscriminating public. This is the characteristic quality of all the early work, most obvious of course where the problem is most difficult. By no means devoid of the beauty that abides in "style," these early tales are nevertheless too rich in matter and ideas to fit themselves easily to a personal diction. Some of them, *The Passionate Pilgrim* in particular, give the impression of a knobby surface of all sorts of thoughts and observations on which the robe of words hangs, not loosely, but with queer misadjustments and places where strain is apparent. It is clear enough that the ideas came first and were of first importance, and that the chief use to their author of lovely words, susceptible as he proved himself to them, was to make his thoughts more clearly perceived, to carry light into the dark depths and make shine the idea found in an obscure corner of the mind.

There was, in a word, nothing dilletante in the earliest product of Mr. James's mind. It was clear enough that he was prepared to probe deeply into the spiritual essence of humanity and that the special and the curious had their charm for him. It was not so clear that he was to throw a vivid light on contemporary manners; and it was not discernible at all, in spite of the fact that many of his characters happen to be Americans in Europe, that the international relation was to furnish him with his most important and sustained theme. It was, however, unmistakable that he was to be a writer dedicated to illumination. The habit of reading him sharpens our capacity for discerning truth. Before he was thirty, he was "striking matches," to use a phrase of his later years, for us to see the finer facts surrounding us: facts of spirit wherever the human comes into play, and in the case of inarticulate landscape, exquisite facts of surface, recognitions of composition and colour in the external world that make in his work a series of pictures so expressively painted as to constitute in themselves a definite achievement for art.

Since his strength was chiefly to lie in combining close observation of the innumerable phenomena of the surface of life with indefatigable exploration of the recondite truths of the spirit, it was his great opportunity to have access to a society permeated by fresh thought and to study that society against the background of the older European civilisation, instead of seeing it within its local limits only. It was his virtue as an artist that he recognised promptly a state of things ready to his hand, a region of manners which he could explore almost as a pioneer, an environment upon which he could steadily draw for animating suggestion. If he was not to conceive a second *Comédie Humaine* his *Comédie Sociale* was, nevertheless, on a scale worthy of a profound student of life. He never committed himself to a plan more vast than he has found it possible to carry on. Certain limitations of taste and interest closed about him at the beginning, and apparently he has never for a moment deviated from the belief so fervently expressed by Joubert and so fervently approved by Arnold, that

with the fever of the senses, the delirium of the passions, the weakness of the spirit; with the storms of the passing time and with the great scourges of human life,—hunger, thirst, dishonour, diseases, and death,—authors may as long as they like go on making novels which shall harrow our hearts, but the soul says all the while, "You hurt me."

Not that these cruelties of human existence have no place in his novels—he would be a strange seeker after the *vraie vérité* who should ignore their presence in the world; but no author ever made them less the reason of his writing, none ever more continually penetrated beyond them to the inner life which is so largely independent of them, none ever more earnestly concerned himself with the ideal and refining elements of human nature while clearly bending a critical vision upon its idiosyncrasies, external and inner.

In his earlier essay on Balzac Mr. James expressed his opinion that only after a man has arrived at full maturity, only after he is thirty, to give a round number to the period, does he produce a thoroughly satisfactory novel. It was in his fourth decade that he himself produced *Roderick Hudson, The American, The Europeans, Daisy Miller, Confidence, An International Episode, Washington Square, The Portrait of a Lady,* and *The Siege of London,* and he had profited by his period of preparation to the extent that none of these show a lack of competence to handle the material or a lack of knowledge of his field, greatly as his capacity was to deepen and broaden with the progress of the pensive years. The first to appear, *Roderick Hudson,* is compactly woven, a tissue of recorded facts in which the pattern of the idea is clearly outlined. A certain conscientiousness of treatment, an absence of improvisation, an obvious desire to make everything clear, to portray convincingly the physiognomies, both physical and mental, of the characters, the particular places in which from time to time they happen to be, their occupations and amusements, above all their relations to one another, is the conspicuous quality in the book, which, in spite of the somewhat formal presentation, so different from the later freedom and luxuriance of metaphor and image, bears a striking likeness to many of its successors. It relates the history of a young sculptor immured in a law office in a New England village and panting for freedom and art. He is rescued by a rich youth who on his side is panting for an opportunity intelligently to do a good deed, and who, recognising the quality of the work produced by Roderick's untrained hand, proposes to supply the needed training in Rome. Roderick, strong in genius, but weak in will and character, falls under the sway of Christina Light, an interesting, death-dealing, irresponsible beauty of whom we hear again in *The Princess Casamassima*. Every part of the story is highly defined and finished with minute detail. We are told a great deal about every one; the history of each character almost from birth is traced with a patient elaboration that reminds us of how often the name of Balzac is mentioned by its author. The principal exhibition is of Roderick's character, allowed to bloom with shattering swiftness in the rich air of the papal city, but each of Roderick's companions also is a concrete human being so visualised as to be entirely recognisable; these, however, vary greatly from one another in interest. A liking, not by any means limited to the early novels, for contrasting brilliant figures with those in which an almost violent reserve, an almost oppressive quietness, is conspicuous, finds expression in the portraits of the two women, Mary Garland and the extraordinary Christina. The former is the dull and colourless forerunner of such exquisitely beautiful creations as Milly Theale, Nanda Brookenham, and the nameless young woman at "Cockers." Perhaps nothing would serve better to mark time and progress than to place one of these perfectly affirmed, delicately represented heroines against the honest and rather heavy image of Mary Garland sitting by her eternal candle busy with her interminable sewing. Mary is what many of her sisters in fiction are: what Laura Pendennis is, with her prayers and tears; what Dinah Morris is, with her cap and reddish hair; what Florence Dombey is, and Lucy, beloved of Richard Feverel, —merely a likeness in monotone of a human figure, essentially human, undeniably real and solid, but without that subtlety of spiritual life to be communicated only by the deepest insight on the part of the artist into the human soul. They are plain "good likenesses" and as such to be treasured in the circle of sitting-room decorations, but none of them is the mysterious evocation of a personality for which lovers of art would cross continents and seas. Christina Light, on the other hand, is a heroine to play her part successfully in any picture at almost any stage of her author's career; a mysterious creature, light and buoyant as a graceful ship just launched, fascinating in her eccentric outline and glowing with physical beauty and charm.

All through the book people explain themselves to each other and explain each other to themselves. All the investigation into character and temperament is done in the open; nothing is concealed; it is easy to follow the mental processes by which the author seeks to make himself "privy to the mystery of knowledge" in all that concerns life, and it would be a rash reader who should deny the special attraction of this slightly clumsy and touching candour of curiosity and effort. There was already the talent noted in the article on Henrik Ibsen, as characteristic of that dramatist's remarkable art—the talent "for producing an intensity of interest by means incorruptibly quiet," by an "almost demure preservation of the appearance of the usual." And there was also an occasional charmed glance at the beauty of the outer world, as in the description of Rowland's walk toward Fiesole, with its quotation from Browning naïvely brought in. There was, moreover, a well-developed plot; a highly professional construction, an ordered drama in which the interest is sharply broken off only to follow the imagination along suggested paths. It was in fact a complete instance of a prophetic achievement. Yet in spite of the fact that Roderick is taken from a Massachusetts village to Rome for his artistic development, we find not more than a phrase or two from which the reader may infer that his tragic history is to mark the beginning of the long series of international dramas. This prophecy may be detected in the account of Roderick's little statuette of a fair youth drinking thirstily from a gourd:

"Tell me this," said Rowland, "do you mean anything by your young Water-drinker? Does he represent an idea? Is he a symbol?" Hudson raised his eyebrows and gently scratched his head. "Why, he's youth, you know; he's innocence, he's health, he's curiosity. Yes, he's a good many things." "And is the cup also a symbol?" "The cup is knowledge, pleasure, experience. Anything of that kind!" "Well, he's guzzling in earnest," said Rowland. Hudson gave a vigorous nod. "Aye, poor fellow, he's thirsty!"

Thirsty America was in the author's mind, no doubt, thirsty then as she is not now for conditions so difficult in that memorable past to attain, thirsty then for ideals of art and culture now cheapened somewhat by their accessibility, and not, apparently, so magical in their allurement. In reading *Roderick Hudson* to-day it is impossible not to let the mind wander from the book to the reality, so close the book obviously is to the reality, and from the past to the greatly different present; it is during these vagrant moments that one perceives how gently the tone of time has descended upon the pages; they have mellowed and taken on a unity of colour and impression that could not have been recognised in them when they came fresh from the press,—the natural effect of age upon the sincere expression of truth in any form of art. What may have seemed a little sharp and thin at the moment it was written is now seen to have conformed to the slightly sharp and thin quality of the scenes and natures described; is seen, too, as the natural note of inexperience, and especially is seen to be the result of the strong sense of responsibility; the instinct of a fine and subtle truthfulness triumphing over a rich imagination in the effort to see life as it is. It was the kind of practice that makes perfect if carried on to the logical end; it was the bondage that makes freedom; it was the attention to truth of substance and truth of manner that makes—in time—beauty.

In *The American*, that followed *Roderick Hudson* after an interval of two years, the step toward beauty is nothing less than a stride. It carries the author, previously punctilious to the verge of stiffness, into flowery gardens of freedom, a freedom marked by his easier handling of his figures, his lightness of touch in manipulating his greater plot, and above all by his manner of good fellowship with his reader, that manner which was to carry him so far in the mystery of style. Already he stood sufficiently aloof from his own country to see the relation borne by the American to the foreigner. The beautiful study of Christopher Newman is accomplished with great simplicity in the mild, winning manner of the later novels. Uncontentious, delicate, generous in his relation towards others, frankly without superficial taste, but with endless inner refinements of kindness and conscience, Newman stands against the background of family arrogance and tradition among the

American Character

French nobility, a presentation of his country's quality such as the unfortunate Roderick might have been proud to equal in a sculptured symbol. The charm of Madame de Cintré, marytred in the great French cause of "family," is no less potent and is communicated by the same mild method. The love of form accountable for the inflexibility of Roderick Hudson had already passed into the flowing expression of culture. Culture, Matthew Arnold has determined for us by two rounded definitions, the familiar "knowing the best that has been thought and known in the world" and the less familiar "getting the power through reading to estimate the proportion and relation in what we read." Whether Mr. James got it through reading or through writing, in *The American* a similar power to realise proportion and relation is present in visible and appreciable shape. It is the first purely artistic result of his passion for artistic embodiment of thought. The care for art in it is extreme, and it is somewhat significant that this early writing has so little of the tremulous sensibility in which youth abounds; and that it has so much painstaking, so much groping concern for propriety of expression, so much careful preparation of the matter. It betrays the fact that the preoccupation of its author with form is not an acquired and grafted characteristic. It was at the beginning his strength and his weakness, yet always more his strength than his weakness. It was the latter in fact only so far as it helped to suppress the expression of a poetic perception as rare as it is exquisite. When in the fire of Spring a young talent is cautious, one too insistently remembers that

> The Bird of Time has but a little way
> To flutter—and the Bird is on the Wing.

It is not, however, to the purpose to think of how a talent would have been had it been different. It is difficult enough to think truly how in itself it is. In the case of Mr. James caution and responsibility fastening themselves on the shoulders of youth surely sufficiently have justified their grasp. The poetry has found its way out and has been perhaps strengthened and enriched by the husbandry that would not let it push prematurely into sight. Self-consciousness with him has passed into poise, cultivation has brought forth luxuriant bloom.

And the fact that he composed from the beginning with his eye "on the object," that he saturated himself from year to year with the experience upon which it was his steady intention to draw for his pictures of life, gave his work the consistent quality of fidelity, the quality that wraps it together. He gave his perceptions that play essential to their growth, recorded the reports they made to him with accurate care, and held himself as disinterestedly as possible in the attitude of a spectator. Full of vitality and curiosity, neither of which apparently has waned in the course of a long service, he curbed his sensibility and the egoism which, since he was young, he must have had, with a remarkable respect for the conditions by which good literature is nourished.

If he was "detached," if he did not give himself away in his books as much as Dickens or Thackeray or George Eliot, he was not less of his race and nation for that. To be transparent, effusive, gushing, he says in his article on Daudet "has never been and will never be the ideal of us of English speech," and the dignity of his early style suggests the normal later flowering in the manner of Anglo-Saxon genius.

The American is the novel which we may take as on the whole perhaps most representative of his early quality, and as in its kind a masterpiece of simple rather than complex art, but unmistakably of art. It contains a number of important characters—none, in fact, that can be called unimportant, so closely is each fitted into the scheme or plot and made to contribute to the development.

Christopher Newman, however, the "American," entirely dominates the interesting group. To him is owing the profound sense of life in the book. If Mr. James did intend, as by the title we are justified in assuming, to make him the image of his country, the concrete representation of an abstraction, he accomplished his object in a way very different from that pursued by other inventors of our supposed type. For one thing, he absolutely refrained from feeding the vanity of his countrymen by making his American an incarnation of a moral or political or national idea. The democratic spirit of Christopher Newman, if by democratic spirit we mean the pride of liberty to do as one pleases without consulting others, is sufficiently obvious; but it is introduced without the tacit glorification of its virtues common to writers of less subtlety and less breeding. "One's theories, after all, matter little," Newman's creator somewhere says in reference to his method of pursuing culture, "it is one's humour that is the great thing." The American's humour is so much the greatest thing about him that, despite his shrewdness, he survives in direct line with Colonel Newcome and the good, dull Dobbin, as one of the gentlest figures in fiction. It was a happy result, the happiest, of an attempt to embody our national characteristic, that, in place of the flamboyant merits on which in literature we have more or less depended for impressiveness, we should see ourselves depicted as possessing the spiritual delicacy ordinarily associated with races of immemorial politeness. Newman has in due degree the idiosyncrasies that make for common recognition of him as an American product. He is a money-maker, who has won his way through difficulties usual enough in the generation of Americans to which he belongs. At the age of fourteen he had been set adrift in the Western world: "necessity had taken him by his slim young shoulders and pushed him into the street to earn that night's supper." It illustrates the choice of adventure commonly made by Mr. James that history begins after the material difficulties are surmounted and the problem has become, how to enjoy the material welfare.

His democracy of enjoyment is a

part of his Americanism. Taking his holiday in Paris he likes the great gilded rooms of his showy hotel; he likes driving rapidly and expensively through the country to see the monuments of history; his ideal of giving a "party" for the celebration of his engagement with the lovely Claire de Cintré is to invite every one who has shown him a minimum of politeness and every one with whom he has a shadow of friendship, and to entertain them with singers and actresses of first quality hired at great cost for the charming and intimate occasion. On the other hand his susceptibility to finer impressions is equally marked, and, with a subtlety of suggestion worthy of the cause, this susceptibility is made to appear also a part of Newman's Americanism, a part so integral as to seem the real essence of everything, the element impossible to change without destroying the organism.

"You are the great Western Barbarian," Mrs. Tristram says to him, "stepping forth in his innocence and might, gazing a while at this poor effete Old World, and then swooping down on it." To this indictment Newman replies with remonstrance. "I am a highly civilised man," he contends, "I stick to that. If you don't believe it I should like to prove it to you." The extent to which he proves it is the psychological basis of the story. The extent of his politeness is the touchstone by which the different characters are tested. If the word appears to minify his frank and sturdy temper it can only be because we allow it a superficial meaning alone and decline to trace it to its deep source in consideration for the comfort of others. At all events, it is clearly enough politeness in Newman that gives him his great air of superiority in the presence of the old French noblesse, and that makes his kind simplicity a force in contrast with their complexity of manner. It is the absence of politeness in the complex Bellegarde manner that constitutes its weakness and converts it by insidious shades into absurdity. It is the politeness of Madame de Cintré that makes her a star of charm in the cold constellation of her relatives, before we are aware of her superior moral virtue. It is the grace of politeness in her younger brother Valentin that makes him the true head of the house of Bellegarde. At the end of the story, which takes, its many readers will remember, a melodramatic turn involving criminal acts and startling disclosures, the politeness by which Newman expresses his rich spirit of benignity blossoms into a state of feeling beside which the cheaper states so frequently encountered both in fiction and in life, seem as tawdry as a milliner's display after the blooming summer hedges. The unfortunate American, duped by his French antagonists, but in possession of their hideous secret for revelation or not as he may choose, has been gazing at the gray walls of the convent to which Madame de Cintré had been driven. Turning away, he walked down to the edge of the Seine and saw above him the soft vast towers of Notre Dame:

He crossed one of the bridges and stood

a moment in the empty place before the great cathedral; then he went in beneath the grossly imaged portals. He wandered some distance up the nave and sat down in the splendid dimness. He sat a long time; he heard far-away bells chiming off at long intervals, to the rest of the world. He was very tired. This was the best place he could be in. He said no prayers; he had no prayers to say. He had nothing to be thankful for, and he had nothing to ask; nothing to ask, because now he must take care of himself. But a great cathedral offers a very various hospitality, and Newman sat in his place, because while he was there he was out of the world. The most unpleasant thing that had ever happened to him had reached its formal conclusion, as it were; he could close the book and put it away. He leaned his head for a long time on the chair in front of him; when he took it up he felt that he was himself again. Somewhere in his mind a tight knot seemed to have loosened. He thought of the Bellegardes; he had almost forgotten them. He remembered them as people he had meant to do something to. He gave a groan as he remembered what he had meant to do; the bottom suddenly had fallen out of his revenge. Whether it was Christian charity or unregenerate good nature—what it was in the background of his soul—I don't pretend to say; but Newman's last thought was that of course he would let the Bellegardes go. If he had spoken it aloud he would have said that he did n't want to hurt them. He was ashamed of having wanted to hurt them. They had hurt him but such things were really not his game. At last he got up and came out of the darkening church; not with the elastic step of a man who has won a victory or taken a resolve, but strolling soberly, like a good-natured man who is still a little ashamed.

This tone of mind, which perhaps we can best define as spiritual courtesy in opposition to the false "politesse stérile et rampante," attaching only to the surface of behaviour, is one upon which Mr. James has continued to bend his discerning gaze. It appears again and again in such diverse individuals as Ralph Touchett, Francie Dosson,

Maisie Farange, Mr. Longdon, Verena Tarrant, Milly Theale, Strether, Adam Verver, and the exquisite Maggie. Although in Newman and in the wonderful late evolution of Newman, Adam Verver, it seems inseparably connected with the nationality of its possessor, it makes its home as well with English Maisie, with Henry Chilver in *The Great Condition*, and with other characters in the short stories that have kept pace with the novels in number, variety and quality. Nevertheless it is true that in nearly all the important American characters the inner delicacy prompting considerate relations with others, the essential kindness seeking happiness in the well-being of others, are so conspicuous as to press upon the reader the conviction that by the writer they are regarded as peculiarly characteristic of his nation. The impression they create is the stronger that Mr. James nowhere shirks his duty as an observer or fails to note the symbols of difference in taste and training which make against the perfection of manner in his national family, as compared with the European tradition. The artistic detachment that has enabled him to record with precision and without prejudice the manners of many countries, has yet left him the ancient right of the artist to add himself to nature in the account of his observations, and there is no injustice to his art in reflecting that he analyses his American characters with a sympathy which lends an ineffable sweetness and warmth to their portraiture. Yet in recognising the elevation of his conceptions of his countrymen and countrywomen it is easy also to perceive that they are not wholly isolated in their essential character. They are the verdant branch of the Anglo-Saxon stock, fed by the same sap that courses through the stout British trunk, if somewhat lighter and gayer and freer in movement, and brighter and thinner in colour, and slighter in form. With what Mr. James somewhere defines as "the faintly acrid perfume of the New England temperament," with sensitive imaginations, fanciful humour, conscientious exclusions and renunciations, they nevertheless are not alien to the English as they are alien to the French and to the Italians. The same taste in morality exists for both. When in *The Golden Bowl* the Roman Prince asks Maggie Verver, who is betrothed to him, if she believes that he is not a hypocrite, if she recognises that he does n't lie or dissemble or deceive, we can imagine the colour rising in an English face as promptly as in hers. The Prince notes, in fact, that the disability seriously to discuss questions of veracity and loyalty or the lack of them is "the English, the American sign," that duplicity, like "love" has to be joked about. The whole matter is put concisely in the following fragment of discourse taken from a very enlightening little paper called *An Animated Conversation*. Several persons, some of them American, the rest English, are exchanging ideas on international differences. The international differences, between England and America, Darcy, an American, characterises as "rubbish," and he holds that if his countrymen are not all "formed," at least they are forming, and on a scale of opportunity like nothing else in the world:

the opportunity for two great peoples to accept, or rather to cultivate with talent, a common destiny, to tackle the world together, to unite in the arts of peace—by which I mean, of course, in the arts of life. It will make life larger and the arts finer for each of them. It will be an immense and complicated problem of course—to see it through; but that's why I speak of it as an object of envy to other nations, in its discipline, its suggestiveness, the initiation, the revelation it will lead to. Their problems in comparison strike me as small and vulgar. It's not true that there is nothing new under the sun; the *donnée* of the drama that England and America may act out together is absolutely new. Essentially new is the position in which they stand toward each other. It rests with all of us to make it newer still.

This was written more than fifteen

years ago and twelve years after the publication of *The American*. The swiftly moving forces of the West already had been hard at work on American civilisation, and already the illusions and ignorances of a Christopher Newman concerning European customs and thought had become of less probable occurrence, had been, at all events, replaced by a different set of illusions and ignorances. Not altogether, therefore, because of their intrinsic worth, but to a large degree because they crystallise for us the evanescent forms of a social state that flowered and withered in a night, must we prize the series of novels executed by Mr. James before the last quarter of the mighty century just closed.

His heroines of that comparatively fresh adventurous time have a serious, simple intensity that makes them beguiling figures in the gravely ordered setting of their lives. Most of them are responsive to new impressions, nervously alive to the interests of the world outside their shuttered windows. Gertrude Wentworth in *The Europeans* meets the impact of foreign life upon her susceptible temperament with sudden tears of joy. Isabel Archer, in *The Portrait of A Lady*, is thrilled with exquisite excitements when she stands for the first time on English ground. They all have firm, clear minds and fine capacities for pure joys and intelligent recreations. They have, too, whatever their age may be, the confiding, idealising tendency of the very young, and a gay perversity, that risks nothing so easily as misunderstanding. The immortal Daisy Miller is the embodiment of the latter perilous attribute and owes her international fame, no doubt, chiefly to the readiness with which she sacrificed to the idol of her American independence. Catherine Sloper, in *Washington Square*, is the one unperceptive intelligence of the group, and her heaviness of mind is adroitly symbolised by her author in the fact that she wears satins at the age of muslins. But she, with the rest, savours of a moral charm composed of two admirable qualities, delicacy and loyalty: these make the little clear flame that burns so steadily beneath all the various exteriors. And as if from the action of this hidden purifying element, the dross of artificial conventions disappears. The moral nature moves with a fine freedom of limb, and the unsophisticated conscience takes unexpected gracious attitudes.

No writer has been more haunted by the compatibility of gentleness with the firmer qualities of the spirit. In Verena Tarrant of *The Bostonians*, it constitutes the invincible charm of an otherwise undistinguished character—unless it be distinguished to have the gift of eloquent, excessive, persuasive speech. The lack of gentleness in her militant companion, Olive Chancellor, is the undoing of an otherwise estimable lady; the presence of it again in the noble and affecting portrait of Miss Birdseye lends to her aged aspect an interest greater than any inspired by her dim, disordered activity in the pursuit of human enfranchisement. Her gentleness pervades her earnest, industrious career, and over the scene of her quiet death casts a perfect grace:

> Miss Birdseye's voice was very low, like that of a person breathing with difficulty; but it had no painful or querulous note—it expressed only the cheerful weariness which had marked all this last period of her life, and which seemed to make it now as blissful as it was suitable that she should pass away. Her head was thrown back against the top of the chair, the ribbon which confined her ancient hat hung loose, and the late afternoon-light covered her octogenarian face and gave it a kind of fairness, a double placidity. There was, to Ransom, something almost august in the trustful renunciation of her countenance; something in it seemed to say that she had been ready long before, but as the time was not ripe she had waited, with her usual faith that all was for the best; only, at present, since the right conditions met, she could n't help feeling that it was quite a luxury, the greatest she had ever tasted.

This sympathetic description is in the style of interested personal comment, and so is the later reference to her burial-place:

> Her mortal remains were to be committed to their rest in the little cemetery at Marmion, in sight of the pretty sea-view she loved to gaze at, among old mossy headstones of mariners and fisher-folk. She had seen the place when she first came down, when she was able to drive out a little, and she had said she thought it must be pleasant to lie there. It was not an injunction, a definite request; it had not occurred to Miss Birdseye, at the end of her days, to take an exacting line or to make, for the first time in eighty years, a personal claim. But Olive Chancellor and Verena had put their construction on her appreciation of the quietest corner of the striving, suffering world so weary a pilgrim of philanthropy had ever beheld.

In the personal manner, also, are the descriptions of Francie Dosson, in *The Reverberator*, which are little more than suggestive musings on the quality directly displayed by that lovable young American in act and speech:

She thought Delia whipped her up too much, but there was that in her which would have prevented her from ever running away. She could smile and smile for an hour without irritation, making even pacific answers, though all the while her companion's grossness hurt something delicate that was in her.
Francie did not in the least dislike Mr. Flack. Interested as I am in presenting her favourably to the reader, I am yet obliged as a veracious historian to admit that he seemed to her decidedly a brilliant being. In many a girl the sort of appreciation she had of him might easily have been converted by peremptory treatment from outside into something more exalted. I do not misrepresent the perversity of women in saying that our young lady might at this moment have replied to her sister with, "No, I was not in love with him, but somehow since you are so very prohibitive I foresee that I shall be if he asks me." It is doubtless difficult to say more for Francie's simplicity of char-

acter than that she felt no need of encouraging Mr. Flack in order to prove to herself that she was not bullied. She did n't care whether she were bullied or not; and she was perfectly capable of letting her sister believe that she had carried mildness to the point of giving up a man she had a secret sentiment for in order to oblige that large-brained young lady. She was not clear herself as to whether it might not be so; her pride, what she had of it, lay in an undistributed, inert form quite at the bottom of her heart, and she had never yet invented any consoling theory to cover her want of a high spirit.

It will hardly be denied by any attentive reader of fiction, that a peculiar talent is required to endow heroines with this mingled quality of simplicity and kindness without suggesting a state of colourless insipidity, an absence of "brain-stuff," fatal to sustained interest. The fact that these softly innocent American heroines, and even the keenly innocent American heroes, wear their temperament with so distinguished an air proves, certainly, the presence in their author of the peculiar talent, but does it not also prove a certain distinguished charm in the American character which has waited—it had not, to be sure, an excessive period to wait —for the right intérpreter, the interpreter whose condition of rightness has been determined not merely by his natural talent, but by his international experience, his possession of a background for his figures, and a standard of comparison?

Isabel Archer is the most instructed of his young Americans, the most given to introspection and analysis, the least humble in the arms of fortune, yet even her brilliant intelligent personality breathes of a purity that is deeper than the mere natural attribute of maidenhood, a purity that lies at the core of character, and is inexpugnable by experience, however extended into dangerous fields. The connotation of her characteristics suggests the comment long after made by Mr. James upon his renewed impression of the wide New Hampshire landscape, that it insists on referring itself to the idyllic type:

as if the higher finish, even at the hand of nature, were in some sort a perversion, and hillsides and rocky eminences and wild orchards, in short, any common sequestered spot, could strike one as the more exquisitely and ideally Sicilian, Theocritan, poetic, romantic, academic from their not bearing the burden of too much history.

This perhaps is the "note" of American character, as of American landscape. from the point of view of a detached but not denationalised observer. Certainly in the following passage, illustrating Isabel's habit of mind and absorbing interest in the laws of her nature, there is a flavour of New World, of Old World unsophistication:

She had an unquenchable desire to think well of herself. She had a theory that it was only on this condition that life was worth living; that one should be one of the best, should be conscious of a fine organisation (she could not help knowing her organisation was fine), should move in a realm of light, of natural wisdom, of happy impulse, of inspiration gracefully chronic. It was almost as unnecessary to cultivate doubt of oneself as to cultivate doubt of one's best friend; one should try to be one's own best friend, and to give oneself, in this manner, distinguished company. The girl had a certain nobleness of imagination which rendered her a good many services and played her a great many tricks. She spent half her time in thinking of beauty, and bravery, and magnanimity; she had a fixed determination to regard the world as a place of brightness, of free expansion, of irresistible action; she thought it would be detestable to be afraid or ashamed. She had an infinite hope that she should never do anything wrong. She had resented so strongly, after discovering them, her mere errors of feeling (the discovery always made her tremble, as if she had escaped from a trap which might have caught her and smothered her), that the chance of inflicting a sensible injury upon another person, presented only as a contingency, caused her at moments to hold her breath. That always seemed the worst thing that could happen to one. On the whole, reflectively, she was in no uncertainty about the things that were wrong. She had no taste for thinking of them, but whenever she looked at them fixedly she recognised them. It was wrong to be mean, to be jealous, to be false, to be cruel; she had seen very little of the evil of the world, but she had seen women who lied and who tried to hurt each other. Seeing such things had quickened her high spirit; it seemed right to scorn them.

If this special psychological charm is notable and typical in the early books it is not less so in the late ones,—*The Ambassadors* and *The Golden Bowl*. Mamie Pocock has it in spite of her largeness, her chattiness, her polysyllables, and the complexities of her hair. Maggie Verver has it to a far more intense degree; in her, it is the finest distillation of delicacy, idyllic, if you will, and Sicilian, but, above all, American.

"There are things, my dear," Mrs. Assingham explains to her husband, "—have n't you felt it yourself, coarse as you are?—that no one could tell Maggie. There are things that, upon my word, I should n't care to attempt to tell her now."

The Colonel smoked on it. "She 'd be so scandalised?"

"She 'd be so frightened. She 'd be, in her strange little way, so hurt. She was n't born to know evil. She must never know it."

Different as the "style" of Maggie's portraiture is from that of Francie, Gertrude, and Isabel, the likeness common to them all is not to be mistaken, and marks for their author's position as a novelist the creation of a special type, and a type, moreover, that has appeared before in fiction only in scattered examples. It has had no place as the central conception of a body of literature; for the illustration of which psychologic detail is gathered, but which is never subordinated or contradicted. It has never before been used as the moral value against which all the minor forms of vice show as motes in a clear light, and all the greater forms as dusky shadow from which such light has been withdrawn.

That it is the American type is

hardly to be made a matter of pride with us, is much more to be made a matter of shame in the degree to which we manage to depart from it; but it is in the nature of a positive joy to reflect in its presence on the amount of intellectual and spiritual experience possible to so finely absorbent a texture. Almost the last word concerning it is said in answer to the perceptive Prince of *The Golden Bowl:*

"You Americans are almost incredibly romantic," he exclaims.

"Of course we are. That is just what makes everything so nice for us."

"Everything?"

"Well, everything that's nice at all. The world, the beautiful world—or everything in it that *is* beautiful. I mean we see so much."

II

A NOVELIST with this strong sense of the poetic element in human nature, and with a tendency to let his imagination wander into the region of mysticism and to interrogate the soul rather than the mind, needs a strong counterbalance of interest in the exterior world to keep his feet firmly on the earth, and to provide for his characters a credible, tangible environment.

In the case of Mr. James, this interest manifests itself as a notable, a truly remarkable, feeling for houses and their furnishings and surroundings, especially where they have the ingratiating touch of age, and an intimate association with the lives of their owners. He feels the genius of places, the inner life behind the outer aspect of ponderable things, and so closely adjusts his vision to fine discriminations in these that the places he knows and likes the best are a part of his drama, a part of the expression of his characters, and even, by a stretch of imagination, are in themselves characters, of an individuality not easily to be forgotten. In the earlier work they live chiefly, however, as a means of expression. The home of the Wentworths, for example, in *The Europeans*, is not only an admirable type of the dwellings of well-to-do Americans of the time and locality indicated, but in its clean, bare formality is precisely the harmonious setting for their serious, open lives:

The doors and windows of the large square

house were all wide open, to admit the purifying sunshine, which lay in generous patches upon the floor of a wide, high, covered piazza adjusted to two sides of the mansion —a piazza on which several straw-bottomed rocking-chairs and half a dozen of those small cylindrical stools in green and blue porcelain, which suggest an affiliation between the residents and the Eastern trade, were symmetrically disposed. It was an ancient house—ancient in the sense of being eighty years old; it was built of wood, painted a clear, faded grey, and adorned along the front at intervals, with flat wooden pilasters, painted white. These pilasters appeared to support a kind of classic pediment, which was decorated in the middle by a large triple window in a boldly carved frame, and in each of its smaller angles by a glazed circular aperture. A large white door, furnished with a highly polished brass knocker, presented itself to the rural-looking road, with which it was connected by a spacious pathway, paved with worn and cracked but very clean bricks. Behind it there were meadows and orchards, a barn and a pond; and facing it, a short distance along the road, on the opposite side, stood a smaller house, painted white, with external shutters painted green, a little garden on one hand and an orchard on the other. All this was shining in the morning air, through which the simple details of the picture addressed themselves to the eye as distinctly as a "sum" in addition.

And in *The Bostonians*, the home of Olive Chancellor, on Charles Street, successfully completes the image of that young woman's exacting temperament as Basil Ransom is first introduced to it.

The general character of the place struck him as Bostonian; this was, in fact, very much what he had supposed Boston to be. He had always heard Boston was a city of culture, and now there was culture in Miss Chancellor's tables and sofas, in the books that were everywhere, on little shelves like brackets (as if a book were a statuette), in the photographs and water-colours that covered the walls, in the curtains that were festooned rather stiffly in the doorways.

Not less representative, in the same book, are the long, bald rooms, in which Verena Tarrant's audience is gathered, and the hot little dining-room of the Tarrant homestead, with its smell of kerosene, its coloured table-cloth, and creaking, unstable chairs.

But it is not until we get away from America, and into England, Italy, and France with Mr. James, that we realise the pervasive influence of beauty and romance in homes, gardens, churches, and little inns; of the mellow bloom imparted by gathered years to the common substances of brick and stone and wood. For the English scene, steeped in its recognitions of an immemorial history, his feeling deepens to inalienable affection. His early impression is recorded in his early story so felicitously named *The Passionate Pilgrim:*

Just the scene around me was the England of my visions. Over against us, amid the deep-hued bloom of its ordered gardens, the dark red palace, with its formal copings and its vacant windows, seemed to tell of a proud and splendid past; the little village nestling between park and palace, around a patch of turfy common, with its tavern of gentility, its ivy-towered church, its parsonage, retained to my modernised fancy the lurking semblance of a feudal hamlet. It was in this dark composite light that I had read all English prose; it was this mild, moist air that had blown from the verses of English poets; beneath these broad acres of rain-deepened greenness a thousand honoured dead lay buried.

He has kept clear of confusions and blunted outlines. His sentiment for places has never degenerated into that irritating sentimentality which sees all beauty under one obliterating light of egoistic fancy. The light of his Italy is never the light of his England; the light of his England is as far as possible removed from that of his America. His Paris haze is possessed of an entirely different personality from his London fog; he respects the facial idiosyncrasies of an English country-house or an Alpine hostelry with as much honourable exactitude as the great portrait painters have employed in the service of their sitters. It is this feeling for shades of truth in its every æsthetic form that makes him a writer so to be depended upon by the untravelled. If from his writings they have not the place itself they at least have an impression of it that has not been falsified in tone or colour by any attempt to fit it to fine language or "arrange" it according to a personal recipe of arrangement.

And if one does not always love the company he keeps, one can hardly fail of love for the places in which he keeps it. *The Portrait of a Lady* is the first of the novels to take us into the familiar life of an old English country-house. The description of Gardencourt, with which the book opens expresses the quality produced by the sense of property, of ownership, of vested rights:

> It stood upon a low hill, above the river—the river being the Thames, at some forty miles from London. A long gabled front of red brick, with the complexion of which time and the weather had played all sorts of picturesque tricks, only, however, to improve and refine it, presented itself to the lawn, with its patches of ivy, its clustered chimneys, its windows smothered in creepers. The house had a name and a history; the old

gentleman taking his tea would have been delighted to tell you these things: how it had been built under Edward the Sixth, had offered a night's hospitality to the great Elizabeth (whose august person had extended itself upon a huge, magnificent, and terribly angular bed which still formed the principal honour of the sleeping apartments), had been a good deal bruised and defaced in Cromwell's wars, and then, under the Restoration, repaired and much enlarged; and how, finally, after having been remodelled and disfigured in the eighteenth century, it had passed into the careful keeping of a shrewd American banker, who had bought it originally because (owing to circumstances too complicated to set forth) it was offered at a great bargain; bought it with much grumbling at its ugliness, its antiquity, its incommodity, and who now, at the end of twenty years, had become conscious of a real æsthetic passion for it, so that he knew all its points, and would tell you just where to stand to see them in combination, and just the hour when the shadows of its various protuberances—which fell so softly upon the warm, weary brickwork—were of the right measure.

In the later novels these careful enumerations give way to the freer movement of a more distinguished style; but the sensitiveness to impressions of ordered humanised habitations, made beautiful by the hand of man, persists; especially the classic element in places, the quality of measure and restraint, finds more and more fervent appreciation. In the earlier though not in the earliest books the romantic and picturesque side of life receives a certain amount of notice. In the London of *The Princess Casamassima* are even nooks and byways that add to the suggestion in that book of a momentary inclination toward the art of Dickens, on the part of the author, a queer plunge into the region of the grotesque. The miserable room in which the crippled sister of Paul Muniment holds her fantastic court, touched with its quaint charm compounded of pitiful gay suggestions; the pink dressing-gown so becoming to the cripple's complexion; the multitude of enlivening prints on the walls; the gaudy variegated counterpane; then, too, the dark prison to which Hyacinth Robinson is carried by his foster-mother for his final ignorant, haunting visit to his real mother, hideously immured there; the little sordid house in Lomax Place,—all these show something of the salient quality, the heightened colour, the touch of strangeness to be found in such luxuriance on the pages of *Little Dorrit* and *Great Expectations*.

When, however, we reach the years signalised by *The Spoils of Poynton*, *The Sacred Fount*, *The Golden Bowl*, the years in which Mr. James defines himself in his work as "a man habitually ridden by the twin demons of imagination and observation" and "never enough for his own peace out of anything," we find a change in the character of the scenes presented, a hint that the tranquillising element of order in beauty has become for him too valuable a property to be dispensed with under whatever pressing urgency of the exceptional and curious. Or perhaps it would be a truer statement to say that his interpretation of the "grand manner," in places as in character offers a more positive revelation of the side of his mind that escapes into the Hellenic spirit for its relief from "the weary weight of this unintelligible world." In such a description as that of Newmarch in

The Sacred Fount, the tortured real is corrected by the calm ideal, and abstract synthetised beauty hangs like a brooding angel over the tangled human spectacle:

There was a general shade in all the lower reaches—a fine clear dusk in garden and grove, a thin suffusion of twilight out of which the greater things, the high tree-tops and pinnacles, the long crests of motionless wood and chimnied roof, rose into golden air. The last calls of the birds sounded extraordinarily loud; they were like the timed serious splashes in wide, still, water, of divers not expecting to rise again. I scarce know what odd consciousness I had of roaming at close of day in the grounds of some castle of enchantment. My few steps brought me to a spot where another perspective crossed our own, so that they made together a verdurous circle with an evening sky above and great lengthening, arching recesses in which the twilight thickened. Oh, it was quite sufficiently a castle of enchantment, and when I noticed four old stone seats, massive and mossy and symmetrically placed, I recognised not only the influence, in my adventure of the grand style, but the familiar identity of this consecrated nook, which was so much the type of all the bemused and remembered. We were in a beautiful old picture, we were in a beautiful old tale, and it would n't be the fault of Newmarch if some other *carrefour*, not far off, did n't balance with this one and offer the alternative of niches in the greenness, occupied by weather-stained statues on florid pedestals.

The consummate felicity of such a picture is the natural outcome of an inextinguishable zest in the writer for art in which the qualities of grace and largeness and discretion are conspicuous. Antiquity in these lovely landscapes "awakes and sings," with a classic note. Where the classic note is impossible, there is still the suggestion in all the pleasant places of an aspect unmeretricious and sincere, as in the dower house at Plash, with its bright, durable, sociable air; its air of "being meant for daily life, for long periods, for uses of high decency." When one comes upon an English drawing-room, it is invariably the picture composed for the intelligent recognition of the artist's eye that meets one. What, for example, could be more reminiscent of some rich example of Venetian painting than the room at Stayes, in that gem of the story-teller's art, *The Liar?*

Oliver Lyon took but a few steps into the wide saloon; he stood there a moment looking at the bright composition of the lamp-lit group of fair women, the single figures, the great setting of white and gold, the panels of old damask, in the centre of each of which was a single celebrated picture. There was a subdued lustre in the scene, and an air as of the shining trains of dresses tumbled over the carpet.

The separate units of these big, unified impressions also are lovingly defined as part of the beautiful world in which we Americans "see so much." It is novel in our fiction to find so much attention paid to what the conventional moralist is bound to regard as trivial accessories of life, and we of the race of Waymarsh are even inclined to look with suspicion on such a profusion of æsthetic detail.

In this field it is quite conceivable that Mr. James may have learned his lesson from Balzac, but only a profound interest in the agreeable subject could have carried him so far. There is hardly a book — early or late — of his in which we do not pass through rooms filled with precious bibelots, veritable *morçeaux de musée*, treasures of passionate collectors, triumphs of texture, surface, colour, and modelling. In *The Portrait of a Lady*, we see the darker side of the dilettante spirit, which flowers obnoxiously in Gilbert Osmond's arid mind. In *The Spoils of Poynton*, the human figures grow dim and wavering in the presence of fresh old tapestry and deep old damasks, old golds and brasses, ivories and laces. In *The Golden Bowl*, the collection of Adam Verver and his infallible authority lend an air of high distinction to the drama played out among objects of such inestimable beauty and value.

All of which for the uninitiated is a tremendous education, a saturation in subtle appreciations that can have but one result—that of quickening interest in all that man has beautified, and of quickening resentment of the much that man has done to vulgarise and debase.

And for the initiated the pleasure is still keener, since the commerce of beauty-loving minds is a revel in æsthetic rapture. It is not until Mr. James returns to America, to receive there, after his many years of absence, his "Autumn impressions," that we realise, and undeniably with a pang, the truth of the ancient saying, that we cannot have our cake and eat it too. He has fed us with the great rich cake of art, and the response of our palate to the delicious flavour has been keen and constant; but when, as in the rural communities of New England, he is compelled reluctantly to "fall back on the land," frankly confessing to the sense of starvation accompanying the act; when we learn from him that the adventure on this occasion of finding in the wilderness a house containing examples of Manet, Degas, Monet, Whistler "made everything else shrivel and fade," that it was "like the sudden trill of a nightingale, lord of the hushed evening," we are suddenly and lugubriously aware that the attention he has given to the cultivated scene has worked for many years against his paying any attention at all to the scene of which tonic wildness is the essence. Yet few writers in all the world and all the ages could be trusted so implicitly with a sunset or a dawn, with the ocean or the sweet, wild fields. How little their poignant poetry would suffer from his discriminating touch is attested by his rare references to the lonelier aspects of nature. The perfect expressiveness of these stirs in the mind a rebellious, an ungracious regret that, having given us so much, he could not give us all. As an irritating, stimulating proof of what he could have done for the lovely, careless land of ours and his, he has scattered over the pages published during his visit here jewels of description for the decoration of his autumn tour. This of the charming Berkshire hill-country:

> The grand manner was in the winding ascent, the rocky defile, the sudden rest for wonder, and all the splendid reverse of the medal, the world belted afresh as with purple sown with pearls—melting, in other words, into violet hills with vague white towns on their breasts.

And of the noble Saco valley, where, for a moment at least, curious question of human documents seems to drop even for so faithful a student, who has sacrificed, since sacrifice of one kind or another was inevitable, the frequency of his interrogation of the soul of nature:

I went down into the valley—that was an impression to woo by stages; I walked beside one of those great fields of standing Indian corn which make, to the eye, so perfect a note for the rest of the American rural picture, throwing the conditions back as far as our past permits, rather than forward, as so many other things do, into the age to come. The maker of these reflections betook himself at last, in any case, to an expanse of rock by a large bend of the Saco and lingered there under the infinite charm of the place. The rich full lapse of the river, the perfect brownness, clear and deep, as of liquid agate, in its wide swirl, the large indifferent ease in its pace and motion, as of some great benevolent institution smoothly working; all this, with the sense of the deepening autumn about, gave, I scarce know what pastoral nobleness to the scene, something raising it out of the reach of even the most restless of analysts. The analyst, in fact, could scarce be restless here; the impression, so strong and so final, persuaded him perfectly to peace. This, on September Sunday mornings, was what American beauty *should* be; it filled to the brim its idea and its measure,—albeit Mount Washington, hazily overhung, happened not to contribute to the effect. It was the great, gay river, singing as it went, like some reckless adventurer, good-humoured for the hour and with his hands in his pockets, that argued the whole case and carried everything assentingly before it.

Not all the references are as happy as these, or as full of the splendid and tranquil joy of the season. Readers of the "Impressions," will not have missed in them the frequent mention of taste, the frequent assumption of it in the land itself, its natural arrangement, its recondite suggestions of drawing-rooms, and dining-tables. These are vagaries of instinct, noted only as determining the individual bent of the writer's mind away from the uncivilised and uninhabited, that make one realise how familiarity may breed, not, indeed, contempt, but its opposite in certain exclusive sympathies and appreciations. The whole explanation lies, perhaps, in the question following one of the freer—one of the perfect passages of description:

> Did one by chance exaggerate, did one rhapsodise amiss, and was the apparent superior charm of the whole thing mainly but an accident of one's situation, the state of having happened to be deprived to excess —that is, far too long—of naturalism in *quantity?* Here it was in such quantity as one had n't for years had to deal with; and that might by itself be a luxury corrupting the judgment.

For the American reader it is the rhapsody that attests a judgment still uncorrupted, and a taste for the purest in "style," and that makes the covetous wish that a writer so equipped with the faculties of observation and reflection could oftener have looked upon "nature unadorned," to record its richer suggestions.

III

But we have gained from this long relinquishment of "naturalism," no doubt, the sense, quite as valuable and perhaps more persistently interesting, of civilisation and the presence of wealth.

In all the work of Mr. James we are conscious of a massive material splendour against which are thrown the shimmering reflections of character and temperament. However elusive these may be, the world we see about us is firm and rich as cloth of gold; and while money is infrequently given a prominent place in the discussion of human experience, the results of large, of immense expenditures are everywhere. The wealth of centuries is distilled in these wonderful houses, these private galleries of priceless art, these scattered, precious objects; while the magnificence of the social scale, the innumerable festivities, the vast, if not entirely noble hospitality, speak of great present incomes and a lavish disposition of them. The mere impression of assimilated and inexhaustible material resources is not, however, so uncommon in English fiction as to be especially worthy of note, unless with it we are shown a mode of thought or an attitude of mind to which the possession and consciousness of wealth bears an intimate relation.

It is not important in a world of acts and motives that people have money: it is greatly important what they do with it, and how they think of it, how it influences their lives and the lives of others. What is the temper of Mr. James's characters toward the solid substance of their fortunes, often of such heroic proportions? Do they hoard it, do they spend with lack of thrift, do they give it away? It is suggestive to reflect that in the case of the Americans they chiefly give it away. In *The Portrait of a Lady*, that story of multitudinous threads, the attitude of Isabel Archer toward her inherited means indicates how literally, for her, money is means, the means in this instance of endowing a scoundrel,—but that is a matter apart. After receiving her uncle's legacy the question at once became how to get rid of it. But for her money she would not have married as she did:

At bottom her money had been a burden, had been on her mind, which was filled with the desire to transfer the weight of it to some other conscience. What would lighten her own conscience more effectually than to make it over to the man who had the best taste in the world? Unless she should give it to a hospital, there was nothing better she could do with it; and there was no charitable institution in which she was as much interested as in Gilbert Osmond. He would use her fortune in a way that would make her think better of it, and rub off a certain grossness which attached to the good luck of an unexpected inheritance. There had been nothing very delicate in inheriting seventy thousand pounds; the delicacy had been all in Mr. Touchett's leaving them to her. But to marry Gilbert Osmond and bring him such a portion—in that there would be delicacy for her as well.

In *The Bostonians* the same hesitation to enjoy the sweet fruits of prosperity is conspicuous in the attitude of Olive Chancellor toward the "elegant home" to which her cousin makes brazen reference: "Do you make it a reproach to me that I happen to have a little money?" she bitterly asks, "The dearest wish of my life is to do something with it for others—for the miserable." The kind old father in *The Reverberator* is a helplessly moneyed person, but, once having made his fortune, the last thing that occurs to him is the desirability of keeping it. His prospective son-in-law announces to him his own disinherited state:

"I ought to let you know," he says, "that my father now declines to do anything for me."
"To do anything for you?"
"To give me any money."
"Well, that makes me feel better," said Mr. Dosson.

"There 'll be enough for all—especially if we economise in newspapers," Delia declared, jocosely.

To have "enough for all" appears to be the financial ideal of the American parent, as Mr. James conceives him: this seems to him the chief use of his millions. Adam Verver, in *The Golden Bowl*, plans, to be sure, an investment of his wealth unsurpassed in "style" by the methods of the Renaissance princes. What could be more definitely in the "grand manner" than his fastidious search for *morceaux de musée*, his odyssey for the love of stainless trophies, his willingness in the presence of superior value to "give the price," yet the conscious motive of his life is accumulation for the sake of bestowal; for the final enrichment of American City, the place where he started in business and toward which, characteristically, he feels a sentiment of indebtedness, a desire to make up to it for having benefited him. And "his easy way with his millions," it is thrown out, taxes to small purpose, in the case of the legal arrangements for his daughter's marriage, the principle of reciprocity. The beautiful heroine of *The Wings of the Dove* has even an easier way with *her* millions, a way so easy that mere death is made to seem a small price to pay for a piece of beneficence so "good" in the collector's sense as that with which she proposes to cap her accumulations of kind attentions to her fellow mortals.

In choosing this mild, beneficent type to represent the "successful person" so prominent in his native country,

Mr. James has carried on his predilection for that quality in character which, like culture, is the most easily recognisable and the least easily defined. Like culture it suggests perfection as "an inward condition of the mind and spirit" and is wholly independent of outward circumstances. "Delicacy" is a word too light and frail and unimportant to carry its mysterious significance. It haunts the spiritual kingdom of his men, his women, and his children; if it is present, beauty is present; if it is absent, all ornamental attributes wear the aspect presented to Maggie Verver by the Golden Bowl after its connection with her unhappiness has been discovered: "As a 'document,' somehow, it was ugly, though it might have a decorative grace."

It is not, however, to be inferred that Mr. James confines his observation of the moneyed class to the dozen or more delightful persons for whom their money is the ripest of opportunities to display their indifference to it save as the medium of sweet charity. The attitude borne by his characters toward their possessions is always implicitly if not explicitly indicated and has as many variations as the members of the human family show in their manner of holding themselves, of walking, of eating, or of dressing. The gross, careless, stupid way of expenditure takes its place in the total effect; the way of the Brigstocks in *The Spoils of Poynton*, with their tragically hideous house, "perversely full of souvenirs of places even more ugly than itself and of things it would have been a pious duty to forget," their love of the polish that is put on with a brush, their avidity and lack of æsthetic standard: the immoral way of poor Maisie's various guardians, marked by the money-hunger of depraved appetites; the immoderate, insolent way of a society in which hostesses and guests are perpetually occupied with casting big nets for large, unintelligent fish, in which the poor are at the mercy of the opulent and pay with their pride —as at Nundham—where they do not pay with their money; and the merely sumptuous, liberal way of such places as the scene of *The Sacred Fount*, where the writer of the story reflects that he and his companions were so fine and formal that the summer stars called to them in vain—"We had ignored them in our crystal cage, among our tinkling lamps; no more free really to alight than if we had been dashing in locked railway train across a lovely land."

The one point usually made in one way or another, directly or by contrast, is that money spells opportunity. "What do you mean by rich?" old Mr. Touchett on his death-bed inquires of his son, "I call people rich," Ralph responds, "when they are able to gratify their imagination." With this superb definition of wealth to start with, much may be done in tracing its correspondence to the actual use of money in life. In nearly all the novels an important part of the web is furnished by the ability or inability of the characters to gratify their imagination. Occasionally that faculty fattens on diet of the sparest, as in the case of the telegraph operator at Cocker's who enters the homes of luxury vicariously through the telegrams coming in from all sides upon her, bringing her bits of the great life on every hand. Less rarely it takes an immense amount of wealth to furnish a very small imagination. As a rule, too, the pinched, cramped, toiling characters depicted in a few scattered instances rejoice in the existence of money in the world, boast an intuitive knowledge of the joys made possible by it, and find their satisfaction in dreaming of lives controlled by opulent circumstances. It was because Hyacinth Robinson in *The Princess Casamassima* was the child of a member of the aristocracy, we must infer, that he felt the tug of his heritage of fastidious tastes and interests, but the old dressmaker, who rescues him from the gutter, feels a glory in his lineage sufficient to eclipse entirely in her mind the shame of it, and Rosy Mumiment, the sister of the socialist, and, from the worldly standpoint, altogether the most hopelessly afflicted member of the *dramatis personæ*, visits upon her brother ridicule and reproach for his antagonism toward the "upper classes." This, no doubt, is a rather fine frame of mind. It has, at all events, the air of dignity inseparable from an ungrudging willingness to recognise superiority without cringing, even where the superiority is a purely material asset. The opposite frame of mind is shown, as if for the value of contrast, in one conspicuous instance, that of Kate

Croy's unscrupulously abject family in *The Wings of the Dove*. Here are the cringing and the overbearing spirit in cheerless union. The crumpled, soiled and undistinguished poverty of Marian Condrip's much-mismanaged home flaunts itself like the flag of pestilence to the recognition of the reader. Her "touchiness" on the subject of her disagreeable dwelling and unpolished little ones prepares the mind for the absence of self-respect in her attitude toward wealth, her abasement before possible means of revenue. Her mother had instilled into her mind early in life the proper mental relation to a rich Aunt. To be wounded and stiff while accepting—this was the mark of the genuine pride of poverty: "The little she offered was to be accepted under protest, yet not, really, because it was excessive. It wounded them—there was the rub!—because it it fell short."

For this type, and for this alone, Mr. James has an almost invidious touch. Generously as he treats all members of the human family who in either their intellectual or moral outlook show a trace of nobility, for the people who grovel he makes not even the apology of the creator to whom nothing he has created is alien. The story of Kate Croy and Milly Theale is fairly divided among those whose attitude toward money is their distinction. Grovelling, brutality, and generosity are all freely exhibited, and the ill-spenders and ill-keepers are, together, as in Dante's *Inferno*, scuffling over a fair world lost. The tissue of sordid hopes, ignoble schemes, monstrous treacheries, would be the dreariest product of the human imagination, not even to be surpassed by the *Cousin Betty* of Balzac, were it not for the spirit of the "Dove," hovering in pity and tenderness over a world of penury and envious desire. This, to be sure, is saying that life without goodness would be all evil, but with Mr. James the evil is seldom so unmitigated as in this case by triturations of the good. Of the taste defined by the French as the prompt ability to discern the presence of beauty amid defects he has so much that we are seldom confronted in his work with more than a fragment of purely vicious human nature. Even of poverty *as* poverty, of the ugly, grim, dismal side of it, there is little. In his total view of life he is inconclusive in that direction. It is not easy to gather from him that he is curious about the desperately downtrodden and helplessly unfortunate. In *The Princess Casamassima*, a book entirely dedicated to the violent social inequalities of a great civilisation, he throws over the scene a light so complex as to be merely bewildering. Carefully as the field is studied there is an absence of concentration, a faltering in message, a sense of confusion, and, one is tempted to suspect, a possible lapse of interest, as if the writer were not wholly won by his theme. The gulf between the heights and depths of London life in its extreme variations is perhaps too great to be bridged in any one novel, especially by an author for whom the smallest problem of our involved human relations presents innumerable gradations and shades to be taken account of in the artistic solution. It is in *The Princess Casamassima*, however, that he introduces Millicent Henning, the big, joyous symbol of the energetic, capable working-class, the most vivid to be found in fiction. No other portrait of a member of this much-depicted class awakens such a sense of life and movement, of health and powers in full activity. Millicent is fine and bold and big of bone, loud-voiced and cheap in taste, fearless, fresh, and beautiful. Her vulgarity is faced with a courage equal to her own; but we think of her finally as something pleasant to remember, something like a swift rush of air through close rooms, like vivid blossoms set in dingy window casements. Her image is as far as possible from the type of failure; is quite, within its range, the type of success in its abounding physical vigour, its strength of growth and coarseness of texture, its freedom and conventionality, its worldliness and honest kindness. Here, certainly, the author was interested, we may freely imagine, even captivated by the bloom and brightness of his handsome young subject. He says of her:

She was very handsome, with a shining, bold, good-natured eye, a fine, free, facial oval, an abundance of brown hair, and a smile which showed the whiteness of her teeth. Her head was set upon a fair, strong neck, and her tall young figure was rich in feminine curves. Her gloves, covering her wrists insufficiently, showed the redness of those parts, in the interstices of the numerous silver bracelets that encircled them, and Miss Pynsent made the observation that her hands were not more delicate than her feet. She was not graceful, and even the little dressmaker, whose preference for distinguished forms never deserted her, indulged in the mental reflection that she was common, for all her magnificence; but there was something about her indescribably fresh, successful and satisfying. She was, to her blunt, expanded finger-tips, a daughter of London, of the crowded streets and hustling traffic of the great city; she had drawn her health and strength from its dingy courts and foggy thoroughfares, and peopled its parks and squares and crescents with her ambitions; it had entered into her blood and her bone, the sound of her voice and the carriage of her head; she understood it by instinct and loved it with passion; she represented its immense vulgarities and curiosities, its brutality and its knowingness, its good-nature and its impudence, and might have figured, in an allegorical procession, as a kind of glorified towns-woman, a nymph of the wilderness of Middlesex, a flower of the accumulated parishes, the genius of urban civilisation, the muse of cockneyism. The restrictions under which Miss Pynsent regarded her would have cost the dressmaker some fewer scruples if she had guessed the impression she made upon Millicent, and how the whole place seemed to that prosperous young lady to smell of poverty and failure.

One has the feeling in reading this description that this is the normal outcome of poverty, which is a dragon to be laid low by the sword of boldness, of bravery, of confidence; that it is only potentially a monster and ready at the magic touch of efficiency to throw off its shell and declare itself the radiant godmother of the fairy-tale. And this, we may argue, is the healthy, philosophic mood, removed equally from facile optimism and languid pessimism. It is not, however, the mood commonly displayed by Mr. James toward failure and success. It is, indeed, hardly too bold an inference to draw from the mass of his work that he prefers the former to the latter, but it must be failure that includes success.

It must be failure based on deliberate choice between obvious arrival and subtle detention in the journey toward accomplishment. The artists, writers, the men of business, like Strether, whose moral is that in any affair involving an obligation the saving grace is not to get anything for yourself,—these are the people who stand a little at one side in the novels, connected by a temperamental kinship, and always peculiarly likable, interesting, modest, fine. If they are seldom greatly endowed with the goods of the world they have found their account in riches of the mind and the imagination. They are the types who "gratify their imagination" with a currency somewhat more precious than the coin of the realm; who are positively richer than they could be with that commodity, since the value of most things lies in the amount that has been sacrificed for them. Even Kate Croy, with her developed liking for material things, saw money as a means—a means of obtaining Merton Densher, and it was "on the side of the mind that Densher was rich for her, and mysterious and strong." The side on which in his vacillating, dubious way he becomes rich and strong and mysterious for the reader is a different one; but certainly he is never so much a success as at the moment of his renouncement. Densher, however, is one of the least, as Strether is one of the most, appealing and inspiring images of failure. The great point made by them all as well as by the images of success is that genuine satisfactions are tremendously expensive;

that either in life or art or money they cost prodigiously. And the true favourites of fortune are those who, not "asquint in mind," are moved to spend "with measure." If gold can be made to "drip colour," to use his happy description of St. Marks, Mr. James approves it. If it adds to the richness and comeliness, the comfort and charm of life, it is in the great tradition of wealth, and if not, the wonderful material of riches is merely poured, inexpensively, into a void from which it must again be gathered for fresh permutation.

This is not a new or isolated view of the question of wealth, but one that has been cherished by all philosophers, from the time of the singer of sweet Colonus, who have seen life steadily and seen it whole. The contribution made to it by Mr. James is largely one of the temper in which it is presented; the admirable liberality with which inclusion is made. It is certainly rare for an æsthetic taste so strong and so sensitive to perceive the positive æsthetic value of moral and intellectual visions. It is rare for the temperament of the dreamer and mystic to have so true an intuition for details of form and surface in tangible objects. Appreciation of the two kinds and uses of wealth, the material and the immaterial,—this, perhaps, is the marked characteristic of his representation of society in which the "picture and the idea" are present in such even proportion.

IV

The temper of the dreamer and the mystic united to that of the observer and analyst gives an extraordinary chance for the play of imagination, and imagination, of course, is of the very essence of vital fiction. Without it we may have moral force, conscientious observation and report, even charm and the semblance of life, but we shall not have life itself. The "busy inner world-building power of our minds," continually supported by our experience and the report of our senses, is what makes coherent and sane the "show world" with which, if we happen to be artists, we strive to explain the actualities surrounding us. We all of us, even if we are not artists, have to a certain degree this world-building power; but unless it is present in eminent force in the work of dramatists and novelists we miss from that work the deep, rich flow of character through plastic forms and apparently capricious facts. We miss the compelling sense of reality produced by correspondence between the understanding and things seen. If the objects defined for us by the artist follow the outline of his thought and are expressive of an inner life which he shares with the inexpressive portion of humanity, we recognise them, not as dead symbols, but as quick with the universal pulse. If the men and women placed by him at different angles for our inspection look out of their eyes with suggestions of a personal experience into which we ourselves may enter by the gate of personal interest; if they make us realise perfectly that there are lives other than our own which we may live; other than our own, yet familiar to us so far as we have explored the region of the soul, we know that the world has been enlarged for us and that we have been in the presence not of sterile but of life-producing art; art which, in a word, is at the service of creative imagination.

This is the only test. The questions of method, style, and theory, so deeply important to the artist himself, are only secondarily interesting to the critic. By whatever method of art the sense of life has been produced, if it is there the performance to one degree or another is successful, and by the recognition or non-recognition of it the critic must stand or fall. But if it is there, one most plausibly may argue, it must affirm itself, it is the business of the artist to make it unmistakable. To whom? To all?

We must then limit the province of the artist to the basic type of life, if there be one, the simplicity of which is beyond the recognition of none, otherwise it would be impossible to draw the line. If not for all, for what class of the public should writers write, painters paint, musicians compose, architects build? If we look at art from the socialist's standpoint we may very well insist that its highest form is a universal form from which all classes of mind can get equal pleasure. But if art means to us the extension of our power to link fresh truth to that already within the range of our experience; if it means the binding this and that on every hand to the knowledge of life already possessed; if it means the fusion in one emotion of recognition and surprise, as if in the beings of a new world we should recognise the familiars of the old, obviously we cannot set limits and impose restrictions. If we wish to be let out into a region of new images and fresh feelings, to bar the door is not the effective first step. If, giving ourselves the utmost freedom, however, and making no restrictive demands, we find in the fictitious characters under our observation unreasonableness, lawlessness and incoherence, a want of unifying intelligence behind their activities, of personal feeling behind their exhibited traits, we are justified in doubting their source in a constructive or creative imagination. Are we thus disappointed in the characters Mr. James has made? Are they not stamped with both universal and particular truth, and do they not live as the result of his personal point of view? Are they real and expressive, or are they fantastic and futile, merely literary as opposed to human figures?

The answer to this query is not to be given by the inattentive reader. The fact that Mr. James surrounds his figures with atmosphere; that he forms them by such an expensive process, to use an expression of his own; that he builds them slowly, richly, with accumulations of experience and reflection; that he provides for them a close tissue of relations and contacts,—all this prevents their springing full-grown into our consciousness at the first moment of our knowing them. And we may reflect that this is also true of the people with whom we have had our most enduring relations in the actual world. We must admit, in any case, that such psychologically complex creations as Maisie Farange, Nanda Brookenham, and Maggie Verver are not for a merely bowing acquaintance. In life such an acquaintance would present each of them as a perfectly simple person, as even, perhaps, a trifle dull. To show the amount of colour and tone in these apparently pale intelligences Mr. James interprets with precision and subtlety their shades of feeling, and distils from their character its finest essence. It is possible that short cuts exist for producing the same result, but no short cut known to the novelist as yet has done it. The complexity of the simple is a delicate matter to deal with, and the intellectual instrument can hardly be too delicately used. If, however, the attention of the reader is won, the impression left with him is of a whole and human conception. Dissection into small parts is not the same thing as the putting together of small parts to form a large effect; and a writer of the artistic importance of Mr. James does not, of course, dissect his characters, although the expression is a favourite one with his critics. His process in its elementary stages may be supposed to be not unlike that of almost any artist worthy of discussion. With him, as with others, no doubt, the idea or conception stands in the secret workshop of his mind, a living model, not a mechanical device, fair and thrilling in its free, primal aspect. The point, then, is to reproduce it in the way best adapted to bringing out its characteristic qualities, and this is where artistic theory may come in. The formula for the production of a masterpiece is given, with as much precision as is possible to any formula, in the following passage from *The Tragic Muse*, where Sherringham is visited by a perception of

the perfect presence of mind, unconfused, unhurried by emotion, that any artistic performance requires, and that all, whatever the instrument, require in exactly the same degree: the application, in other words, clear and calculated, crystal-firm as it were, of the idea conceived in the glow of experience, of suffering, of joy.

It is in the glow of experience, of

suffering, of joy, certainly, that the imagination creates its ideal; the rest is workmanship, and the manner of this depends greatly on the fulness of expression desired by the artist. If he begins, as is frequently the case, with a swiftly executed cartoon or sketch of his plan, he almost invariably puts into it a fire and spirit which, with equal certainty, more or less evaporate in the elaborated achievement. A sketch, however, can be only the suggestion, not the realisation of a masterpiece. If we care only for the idea in its simplest aspect, hot from the mind, we may prefer it; but if we care for the value and function of a developed conception, passionately true in outline and modelling to the details of the informing thought, exquisitely filled out and refined, we would hardly choose, if the choice were ours to make, to sacrifice the masterpiece.

If, then, we perceive in such a subject as—in the case of Maisie—the development of the moral sense in a child under the pressure of vice and deception, an idea demanding the subtlest realisation of the actual nature of a child, and if in the accomplished work we perceive the lovely flowering of the tortured moral sense without a strain on the credulity of the reader, we must suppose that the creative imagination has been effectively at work, whether the craftsmanship has shown as loose and free or fine and close and searching.

If in *The Golden Bowl* the moral charm of the theme seems to us to lie in the portrayal of an infrangible innocence of soul to be found at the core of certain natures, and if Maggie Verver, standing light and clear against a background of infinite complication, is the embodiment of that innocence, we must from all experience of art assume that she first appeared to the artist in her gracious integrity, and that the loading of her lovely portrait with significant detail is the mark of his appreciation of how much existed in her to express. She is, in fact, like Maisie and Nanda Brookenham and Mildred Theale, at once a type and a highly specialised individuality. She is a type of the goodness, of the engaging naturalness enhanced and made beautiful by delicacy and warmed by intense responsible affections, for appreciation of which the common world has no sense fine enough. She is not, however, left in the spacious region of the general, where a few largely composed conceptions of human qualities wander about for our easy discernment. She has curious intricacies of feeling and judgment hidden from the casual glance. Her communings and doubtings and believings bring her home to our credence as a person beside whom we have walked, in whom we have lived. No such sense of close familiarity broods over our intercourse with Thackeray's Amelia and Laura Pendennis or George Eliot's Romola and Dorothea and Dinah, who in their way stand also for responsible affections. An imagination of the most vital sort is required for such a scene as that between Maggie and her father, ending in the embrace, "august and almost stern," that sealed the expression of their belief in each other. Not even the frank and tender pathos of Colonel Newcome's relation with his son probes so deeply the heart of the filial instinct. A still broader and swifter movement of the mind is needed for such a scene as that between Maggie and the Prince in the presence of the shattered bowl; for such a scene as the final one between Nanda and Mr. Longdon, or that on which Maisie takes leave of Sir Claude. It is the magic of genius thus to surprise sentiment at its source, and at moments of great moral significance to move the heart with pity.

Ordinarily, writers possessed of the imagination that produces life to a great measure are lacking in decorative fancy. Life is so serious to them even as the subject of satire that the mind declines to play with it, to dress it in costume, and laughingly parade it. Even Thackeray, inveterate joker as he was, could not "have fun with his mind." His fun, where it is not merely the ebullition of high spirits, is too deeply tinged with irony to communicate the pleasure of the game. With Mr. James, however, fancy follows imagination as some fluttering small bird follows, sometimes, perhaps, impeding, the flight of a larger one. In the use of metaphor especially, this swift-circling, darting humour holds the reader fascinated by its unexpected flashings and flexions, and continually entertained by gay parallels and whimsical suggestions. What could be more actively in the comic vein than the reflection on Maisie's first parting from Mrs. Wix? "The child had lately been to the dentist's; she had a term of comparison for the screwed-up intensity of the scene. It was dreadfully silent, as it had been when her tooth was taken out." Maisie herself, between her dreadful parents, is "a ready vessel for bitterness, a deep little porcelain cup in which biting acids could be mixed"; and in her pursuit of an education she goes to lectures where the fountain of knowledge in the form of a high voice plashes "in the stillness of rows of faces thrust out like empty jugs." Lady John's "ornamental information" in *The Sacred Fount* is "as strong as a coat of furniture polish," and that mistress of both culture and slang makes one think of "a hat

askew on a bust of Virgil," while in the same book May Server's bedimmed smile flutters "like a bird with a broken wing." Before the young woman in the "Cage" the gathered bloom of London experience passes at close range—"the nose of the observer was brushed by the bouquet, yet she could never really pluck even a daisy."
The heroine of "Europe" makes her tremendous preparation for a journey to that foreign clime, and her sisters talk of her preparation "as if it were some mixture for application somewhere, that she kept in a precious bottle." Strether, wandering in Paris, has a rich consciousness of time—"a bag of gold into which he constantly dipped for a handful." Strether, again, habitually shakes the bottle in which Life hands him the wine of experience and

finds the taste of the lees rising into his draught. To this guileless American, too, there is something in the great world "covertly tigerish," which comes to him in the charmed air of Gloriani's garden-party as a "waft from the jungle." The Boston lady in *The Wings of the Dove* flits "in and out of the Public Library with the air of conscientiously returning or bravely carrying off in her pocket the key of knowledge itself." In *A London Life* the witty expression of Lady Davenant's face "shines like a lamp through the ground-glass of her good breeding." These copious examples of apt analogy and comparison—one could pluck them thus ruthlessly from their context on nearly every page—give an air of remarkable readiness and brightness to the style. They season it as the best of anecdote seasons talk. They make it as flexible and incidental as talk, and even where they are most like the froth left by the wave of a thought breaking on the mind, they are purely spontaneous and without perversity. They are found in less profusion in the earlier books than in the later, and carry less significance, but even in the earliest they spring up like self-sown flowers in the footprints of experience. In *The Golden Bowl* they take on a more complex aspect and are oftener loaded with a meaning that haunts the mind. Such a figure as that of Charlotte, led through her husband's galleries by a long silken halter looped round her beautiful neck,—Adam's wordless smiles corresponding to soft shakes of the silken rope,—becomes an insistent possession of the reader's thought which follows the unfortunate pair, thus closely held, thus surely separated, to their doom and refuge in American City.

Nor can one easily put out of mind the remarkable image figuring the arrangement by which Maggie had been able to marry without breaking with her past. The beautiful situation,—Amerigo and Charlotte living with Maggie and Adam in intimacy for the admiration of all observers,— the situation so unusual, so liberal, but at the first moment of alarmed insight so baffling, had been occupying the very centre of the garden of Maggie's life;

but it had reared itself there like some strange, tall tower of ivory, or perhaps rather some wonderful, beautiful, but outlandish pagoda, a structure plated with hard, bright porcelain, coloured and figured and adorned, at the overhanging eaves, with silver bells that tinkled, ever so charmingly, when stirred by chance airs. She had walked round and round it—that was what she felt; she had carried on her existence in the space left her for circulation, a space that sometimes seemed ample and sometimes narrow: looking up, all the while, at the fair structure that spread itself so amply and rose so high, but never quite making out, as yet, where she might have entered had she wished. She had not wished till now—such was the odd case; and what was doubtless equally odd, besides, was that, though her raised eyes seemed to distinguish places that must serve, from within, and especially far aloft, as apertures and outlooks, no door appeared to give access from her convenient garden level. The great decorated surface had remained consistently impenetrable and inscrutable. At present, however, to her considering mind it was as if she had ceased merely to circle and to scan the elevation, ceased so vaguely, so quite helplessly to stare and wonder: she had caught herself distinctly in the act of pausing, then in that of lingering, and finally in that of stepping unprecedentedly near. The thing might have

Imagination   165

been, by the distance at which it kept her, a Mahometan mosque, with which no base heretic could take a liberty; there so hung about it the vision of one's putting off one's shoes to enter, and even, verily, of one's paying with one's life if found there as an interloper. She had not, certainly, arrived at the conception of paying with her life for anything she might do; but it was nevertheless quite as if she had sounded with a tap or two one of the rare porcelain plates. She had knocked, in short—though she could scarce have said whether for admission or for what; she had applied her hand to a cool, smooth spot and had waited to see what would happen. Something *had* happened; it was as if a sound, at her touch, after a little, had come back to her from within; a sound sufficiently suggesting that her approach had been noted.

From one point of view such an elaboration of a symbol is fantastic and has in it even an element of perversity. The purely literal reader opening a second volume on such an astonishing passage throws up his hands in despair. "Why not tell us out and out," he says, "that Maggie sees their position to be impossible and is making up her mind to break in on it?" But, as a matter of fact, we are told precisely this "out and out," and we are given the picture besides, to make more vivid our sense of the deep mystery of soul and conscience involved. The very charm of it lies in the fact that we are thrown into a childlike state of wonder at the strange beauties to be found in the course of psychological exploration. From the point of view of one who likes it, such an exercise of the imagination brings back the delicious early sense of living in a fairy-tale, but without the sacrifice of our later sense of reality. We gain from it both the show of things and their significance, both the fable and the moral, both the text and the picture. Reality puts on for us a coat of many colours and shines and shimmers in a hundred lights. The greater writers dear to the English race, Dante and Cervantes and Shakespeare, have chosen the happy road of metaphor and illustration to bring home to us subtle moral conditions, and it is perhaps only a somewhat ponderous taste or a somewhat vain solemnity that fails to enjoy the spring of the intelligence toward a play with toys so precious. At all events, if the fancy of *The Golden Bowl* and *The Wings of the Dove*, with its tossing balls, its rockets and Roman candles, its jewels and chariots, its outfit of a mimic world, does not lighten for us the journey toward truth sitting austere and beautiful at the heart of the maze; if we find triviality in the union of the real and the pictorial; if we have not patience to look at a theme in all its mingled relations and associations and suggestions, we are simply too much out of it for our own pleasure, and there is nothing to do but turn to the thinner medium of pure allegory or the colder medium of literal prose.

V

The only drawback to an eloquent, imaginative style is that it sometimes obscures by its very exuberance of expression the clear philosophic message which from an observer of life and manners we consistently expect. It is perfectly possible with Mr. James to miss his philosophy of life, as more than one critic has demonstrated. It is easy, no doubt, in a wood so closely set with handsome growth, to see only the trees. It may even be difficult, from one or two or three of the novels, particularly the earlier ones, to obtain the synthetic moral effect, the positive moral quality of the theme and its treatment, without which the most ingenious story in the world lacks interest for the Anglo-Saxon reader. But from the work in mass or from any one of the later examples, save, perhaps, *The Sacred Fount*, which savours of ironic pleasantry rather than serious exercise of power,—we can hardly fail to get, in addition to the exhilarating sense of life a sense of the judicial mind back of the performance. Mr. James, in his essay on *The Art of Fiction*, so frequently quoted for and against his method, has laid especial stress on the air of reality, the necessity of successfully producing the illusion of life, but he also, in the same essay, has called attention to "the very obvious truth that the deepest quality of a work of art will always be the quality of the mind of the producer."

In proportion as that intelligence is fine [he says] will the novel, the picture, the statue partake of the substance of beauty and truth. To be constituted of such elements is, to my vision, to have purpose enough. No good novel will ever proceed from a superficial mind; that seems to me an axiom which, for the artist in fiction, will cover all needful moral ground: if the youthful aspirant take it to heart it will illuminate for him many of the mysteries of "purpose."

And while he has said in his essay on Daudet that "life is, immensely, a matter of surface, and if our emotions in general are interesting, the *form* of those emotions has the merit of being the most definite thing about them"; this is more or less in the way of a civil comment on the fact that Daudet sees "mainly the great surface of life and the parts that lie near the surface." Toward the end of the essay he suggests that Daudet's insight "fails him when he begins to take the soul into account," and "that amounts, after all, to saying that he has no high imagination and, as a consequence, no ideas." "Imaginative writers of the first order," he adds, "always give us an impression that they have a kind of philosophy." If we have been interested in the work of Mr. James we are certainly conscious of that impression from it, whether we analyse it or not for ourselves. The reader who considers, not at all as an analyst or a critic, but merely as an interested person, the "tone"—in this instance the moral tone—of his writings, finds it amply composed of moral emotions, preferences, and instincts—just the lack of which in Charles de Bernard caused him to define that writer as second-rate. Not that he puts up sign-posts along the page to show the direction in which he is leading us—there would be something decidedly not in character in the apologetic nature of that method. We must go with him on trust if we go with him at all, but the timid may find in his criticism of other artists plentiful assurance of the high regard in which he holds the moral element of a work of art. Morality, he somewhere affirms, is

simply a part of the essential richness of inspiration—it has nothing to do with the artistic process and it has everything to do with the artistic effect. The more a work of art feels it at its source, the richer it is; the less it feels it, the poorer it is. People of a large taste prefer rich works to poor ones, and they are not inclined to assent to the assumption that the process is the whole work.

This is only one of many utterances that demonstrate his interest in the moral world, but his fullest demonstration of it is in his novels and stories themselves, where his subject is nearly always laid in the depths of human character. His plot turns on how the persons of the drama feel and act in responsible relations. The society in which they move is depicted with true magnificence of detail,—detail with him, as with Mrs. Assingham, finds him and leaves him unappalled and unwearied,—and the correspondence with life is close enough to satisfy the most exacting of realists. In the matter of conversation, for example, the forms of speech are so caught in the fleeting idiom as to make one tremble for their obsolete appearance in the near future. But the "criticism of life" involved in his choice of types, in his delineation of conduct, and the importance he gives to special qualities of mind and heart is what, after all, determines his importance in literature. These are what suggest the moral reality underlying realities of surface. Charming as we might find the detail in *The Golden Bowl*, that work would not be greatly significant to us if what we traced in it were merely the movement of shallow passions and superficial natures. What is important in *The Ambassadors*, back of the truly masterly execution of the difficult theme, is the awakening of Strether to responsibilities of which he has become aware through the irresponsibility of others, and his personal renunciation in obedience to his sense of his own responsible position. What is morally important in *The Awkward Age* is the deep response of

Nanda Brookenham's nature to the refuge held out to her by her grandmother's ancient lover. In *What Maisie Knew* it is not the dreadful items of her knowledge, but the triumph of her beautiful little spirit over their vast sum that gives to the book its moral spring. The artistic process by which these interesting and deeply "moral" persons are placed, surrounded by the "miscellaneous remplissage of life," and helped to their air of verisimilitude by the notation of their various points of contact with other lives, is a matter for discussion by the expert critic, not, certainly, by the amateur reader. The only point properly to be made by the amateur is that an elevated view of conduct appears in Mr. James's novels and is emphasised by the governing reflection that holds together notes of incident and observation. If to have a philosophy of life is, according to the recent definition of a most accomplished critic, "to be profoundly impressed by certain truths," it is pertinent to ask what these truths in the present case are. Among the more obvious is, to use the simplest and most familiar of terms, the beauty of goodness. Since goodness in its latent and hidden and delicate phases is made to play so leading a part, since it is made to comprise so many gracious qualities not always associated with it,—the pretty habit, in Maisie and in Maggie Verver, for example, of making pleasant the paths of their companions by a sweet pliancy of will in matters of personal comfort or choice,—since pride and selfishness and vanity are made ugly not by emphasis and exaggeration, but by mere contiguity with their so much lovelier opposites depicted with persuasive appreciation, we can only infer that goodness in its most pervasive and least aggressive, least alloyed, form presents to Mr. James the appearance of beauty. It may be a question of moral taste or of moral conviction, but the result is the same: the natures that in his novels represent goodness in its purity also represent extraordinary charm. Like the radiant Beatrice they are "exceeding rich in human sympathies," and their exquisite kindness, like the beauty of that fair lady, draws round them the "clear line of love and blessed faith and gentleness."

Not even in these guileless natures, however, is goodness the mere passive preference for amiable acts and attitudes of mind. No truth more powerfully impresses their author, if we may judge from their conduct, than the accountability of human beings to their human quality. The side of human nature which differentiates it from the nature of the lower animals, the side by which people draw profit from the discipline of life, hold themselves up to the requirements of reason, and recognise their responsibility in the moral world, is that on which he most persistently looks. Few of all his novels and stories, and their number has been great, fail to present a problem of choice. The motives are not little, or the solutions mean, although the picture frequently is of a sordid society and a debased code of conduct. The dark side is there in all its darkness, although, of course, the shadow is not unrelieved. Frequently we observe in life that weakness is charming, for example, and many of the weak people drawn by Mr. James are very charming: Vanderbank, Sir Claude, and the Prince—even Chad in *The Ambassadors* has an aspect of charm, which, however, seems to sit superficially upon him and not to belong to his essential temper as with the others it does. But their charm does not save them from the final inference drawn from their histories, that to be strong and reasonable and kind is charming, too, and something more. This, perhaps, is the most vital lesson to be gained from the novels of Mr. James by the people who ask themselves after reading a book how it has made them feel toward life. It is a moral lesson because it proceeds from a profound and definite sense of moral values. It is all the more a moral lesson, one may reasonably suspect, because it is not enunciated with the voice of a teacher for whom art is in a sense a tool of trade, like the old-fashioned ferule or the new-fashioned modelling-clay, but with the voice of the artist for whom his art is his whole expression.

And it is not less impressive because there is so little of the invidious in the attitude taken toward the human spectacle at large. "We are prone to conceive of the ultimate novelist," Mr. James says in his essay on Turgenieff, "as a personage altogether purged of sarcasm." Sarcasm does not, indeed, prevail in his own novels. His treatment of his personages, bad or good, is respectful to the extent, at least, that he takes them seriously, looks deep into their minds, into their souls, and gives them the full benefit of all he finds there. If they are intelligent they cannot complain that he has made them stupid; if they have aspirations and enthusiasms and opinions they cannot bring it up against him that he has missed their point of view. It would be quite absurd to judge his picture of London society—a very important feature of his work—without knowing that society at first hand; but one does not need to be an initiated person to perceive that his ideal of taste for an observer is that of Mr. Longdon in *The Awkward Age*,—an ideal involving an immense effort wholly to understand before pronouncing judgment. It will be remembered that in the case of Mr. Longdon the final result of his understanding was a shouldering of personal responsibility in the excellent tradition of his generation and according to the prompting of his own conscience and taste. Conscience and taste are not so widely separated with Mr. James as with many writers, and especially with many moralists. He puts a great deal of taste into the exercise of his conscience and a great deal of conscience into the exercise of his taste. But taste as he uses it has a somewhat different function from that commonly accorded it. It has both intellectual and moral force, for one thing. It has, to give it the happy definition found for it by Walter Pater in his chapter on *Diaphaneité*, freshness without shallowness, "the range and seriousness of culture without its strain and over-consciousness." With Mr. James, it determines his temper toward the people he criticises and toward the people who criticise him:

however incumbent it may be on most of us to do our duty [he says in his essay on Flaubert], there is, in spite of a thousand narrow dogmatisms, nothing in the world that any one is under the least obligation to *like*—not even (one braces oneself to risk the declaration) a particular kind of writing.

It determines also his attitude toward the "great passions," which are said mainly to be left out of his work. The greatest of them, love, is not so much left out as put in, but oftenest in the guise it takes with responsible persons. In his article on Loti he has told us his opinion about that writer's

almost inveterate habit of representing the closest and most intimate personal relation as unaccompanied with any moral feeling, any impulse of reflection or reaction [and at the same time he adds]: The closer, the more intimate is a personal relation the more we look in it for the human drama, the variations and complications, the note of responsibility for which we appeal in vain to the loves of the quadrupeds.

It is passion on this level that we see in his more distinguished characters, distinguished by the ability to renounce for the happiness of others, and to renounce without bitterness, or to bear without bitterness, if the case require that.

"I can bear anything—for love," the Princess declares in her talk with Mrs. Assingham, when she is first assured that her husband and her father's wife are in love with each other.

> "Of your father?" her friend asks her.
> "For love," she repeats.
> "Of your husband?"
> "For love," she says again.

Later in the book she explains to her father—as only such a daughter could explain to such a father:

"My idea is this, that when you only love a little you're naturally not jealous—or are only jealous a little, so that it does n't matter. But when you love in a deeper and intenser way, then you are, in the same proportion, jealous, your jealousy has intensity and, no doubt, ferocity. When, however, you love in the most abysmal and unutterable way of all—why then you're beyond everything and nothing can pull you down."

This, perhaps, is an Anglo-Saxon form of the "overmastering passion"—it has, at all events, no striking resemblance to that commemorated in the fiction of the Latin races. Its great virtue is the sense it gives of security, of freedom from vicissitude. But whatever its comparative quality it is the inspiration of the characters especially celebrated in the novels of Mr. James, and one at least can say for it that it is a very dignified emotion, which does not interfere with the keeping of laws human or divine. If one cared to carry the "lesson" of *The Golden Bowl* into the region of applied ethics it would be found to emphasise to a degree extraordinary in novels the weight and importance of responsible affection as opposed to the irresponsible elements threatening it, and its highly superior power to uphold and put life into the institution of marriage. The affection of Nanda for Vanderbank in *The Awkward Age* carries with it something of this deep quality, also; it permits her to think for others in their way, so different from her own, and to see, moreover, the rightness of Vanderbank "for himself" in not loving her. This treatment of "questions of the heart" is not conventional or stereotyped, but may it not be said almost in itself to constitute a "philosophy of life" worthy of comparison at least with that of other writers of fiction?

BIBLIOGRAPHY

Compiled by
FREDERICK ALLEN KING

The aim of the present bibliography is to furnish literary guidance. A chronological arrangement has been chosen, bringing each part of the author's work—fiction, essay, or biography—into one logical scheme which exhibits the development of his genius. Reference is made to the periodical giving initial publication and also, where such is the case, to the volume where the story or essay has been reprinted in book form. It has been thought expedient to dispense with the customary spacing of book-titles. Wherever possible, reference is made to the English as well as American editions. It is feared, however, that the present list does not include mention of all the English rearrangements nor the successive reissues of groups of stories, necessary data being unobtainable on this side the ocean.

1865

The Story of a Year. *Atlantic Monthly*, March.

1866

A Landscape Painter. *Atlantic Monthly*, February.
A Day of Days. *The Galaxy*, June. Reprinted in *Stories Revived* (1885).
The Novels of George Eliot. *Atlantic Monthly*, October.

1867

My Friend Brigham. *Atlantic Monthly*, March.
Poor Richard. *Atlantic Monthly*, June–August. Reprinted in *Stories Revived* (1885).

1868

The Story of a Masterpiece. *The Galaxy*, January–February. Illustrated by Gaston Fay.
The Romance of Certain Old Clothes. *Atlantic Monthly*, February. Reprinted in *A Passionate Pilgrim* (1875), also in *Stories Revived* (1885).
A Most Extraordinary Case. *Atlantic Monthly*, April. Reprinted in *Stories Revived* (1885).
A Problem. *The Galaxy*, June. Illustrated by W. J. Hennessy.
DeGray: a Romance. *Atlantic Monthly*, July.
Osborne's Revenge. *The Galaxy*, July.
The Spanish Gypsy. By George Eliot. *North American Review*, October.

1869

Pyramus and Thisbe. *The Galaxy*, April. Comedietta.

A Light Man. *The Galaxy*, July. Reprinted in
  Stories Revived (1885), also *Stories by American
  Authors* (1894).
Gabrielle de Bergerac. *Atlantic Monthly*, July–
  September.

1870

Travelling Companions. *Atlantic Monthly*, November–December.

1871

A Passionate Pilgrim. *Atlantic Monthly*, March–
  April. Reprinted in *A Passionate Pilgrim*
  (1875), also *Stories Revived* (1885).
Still Waters. *Balloon Post* (published at the
  French Fair, Boston, in aid of the destitute
  people of France), No. 2, April 12, 1871.
At Isella. *The Galaxy*, August.
Master Eustace. *The Galaxy*, November. Reprinted
  in *Stories Revived* (1885).
Watch and Ward. *Atlantic Monthly*, August–
  December. Published in book form in 1878.

1872

A Change of Heart. *Atlantic Monthly*, January.
  Comedietta in 15 scenes.
Taine's English Literature. *Atlantic Monthly*, April.
Guest's Confession. *Atlantic Monthly*, October–
  November.

1873

The Bethnel Green Museum. *Atlantic Monthly*,
  January. Criticism of pictures.

The Madonna of the Future. *Atlantic Monthly*, March. Reprinted in *A Passionate Pilgrim* (1875).
Théâtre de Théophile Gautier: Mystères, Comédies et Ballets. *North American Review*, April. Reprinted in *French Poets and Novelists* (1878).
The Sweetheart of M. Briseux. *The Galaxy*, June.
A Roman Holiday. *Atlantic Monthly*, July. Reprinted in *Transatlantic Sketches* (1875).
Roman Rides. *Atlantic Monthly*, August. Reprinted in *Transatlantic Sketches* (1875).
Roman Note Book. *The Galaxy*, November. Reprinted in *Transatlantic Sketches* (1875).
Roman Neighbourhoods. *Atlantic Monthly*, December. Reprinted in *Transatlantic Sketches* (1875).

1874

The Last of the Valerii. *Atlantic Monthly*, January. Reprinted in *A Passionate Pilgrim* (1875), also *Stories Revived* (1885).
A Chain of Italian Cities. *Atlantic Monthly*, February. Reprinted in *Transatlantic Sketches* (1875).
Madame de Mauves. *The Galaxy*, February–March. Reprinted in *A Passionate Pilgrim* (1875).
An Autumn Journey. *The Galaxy*, April.
Frühlingsfluthen. Ein König Lear des Dorfes. Swei Novellen von Iwan Turgeniew. *North American Review*, April.
Siena. *Atlantic Monthly*, June. Reprinted in *Transatlantic Sketches* (1875).
Adina. *Scribner's Monthly*, June–July.
Professor Fargo. *The Galaxy*, August.

Théophile Gautier, Souvenirs Intimes. Par Ernest Feydeau. Histoire du Romantisme, Suivie de Notices Romantiques, etc. Par Théophile Gautier. *North American Review*, October.
Eugene Pickering. *Atlantic Monthly*, October–November. Reprinted in *A Passionate Pilgrim* (1875).
Duke of Montpensier's Pictures at the Athenæum (Boston). *Atlantic Monthly*, November.

1875

Roderick Hudson. *Atlantic Monthly*, January–December. Published in book form in 1876; again in revised form in 1879.
Pictures Lately Exhibited. *The Galaxy*, July. Comments on contemporary American artists.
Benvolio. *The Galaxy*, August.
Tennyson's Drama (Queen Mary). *The Galaxy*, September.
Letters of Madame de Sabran. *The Galaxy*, October. Reprinted in *French Poets and Novelists* (1878).
Le Dernier des Valerius. *La Revue des deux Mondes*, November 15.
The Two Ampères. *The Galaxy*, November. Reprinted in *French Poets and Novelists* (1878).
Honoré de Balzac. *The Galaxy*, December. Reprinted in *French Poets and Novelists* (1878).
A Passionate Pilgrim and Other Tales. Boston: James R. Osgood & Co., (present publisher: Houghton, Mifflin & Co.).

    Contains also: The Last of the Valerii (1874); Eugene Pickering (1874); The Madonna of the Future (1873); The Romance of Certain Old Clothes (1868); Madame de Mauves (1874).

Transatlantic Sketches. Boston: James R. Osgood & Co., 1875 (present publisher: Houghton, Mifflin & Co.).

Contains: Chester (1872); Litchfield and Warwick (1872); North Devon (1872); Wells and Salisbury (1872); Swiss Notes (1872); From Chambéry to Milan (1872); From Venice to Strasburg (1873); The Parisian Stage (1872); A Roman Holiday (1873); Roman Rides (1873); Roman Neighbourhoods (1873); The After Season in Rome (1873); From a Roman Note Book (1872); A Chain of Cities; The St. Gothard (1873); Siena (1873); The Autumn in Florence (1873); Florentine Notes (1874); Tuscan Cities (1873); Ravenna (1874); The Splügen; Hamburg Reformed (1873); Darmstadt (1873); In Holland (1874); In Belgium (1874).

Dates after the titles give the years in which the papers were contributed to *The Nation* and the *Atlantic Monthly*.

Roderick Hudson. Boston: James R. Osgood & Co., 1875 (present publisher: Houghton, Mifflin & Co.).

1876

Le premier amour d'Eugene Pickering. *La Revue des deux Mondes*, January 1.

Minor French Novelists. *The Galaxy*, February Treating Charles de Bernard; Flaubert; MM. de Goncourt. Reprinted in part in *French Poets and Novelists* (1878).

La Madone de l'avenir. *La Revue des deux Mondes*, April 1.

King of Poland and Mme. Geoffrin. *The Galaxy*, April. Criticism of their correspondence.
The American. *Atlantic Monthly*, June–December; 1877, January–June.
Crawford's Consistency. *Scribner's Monthly*, August.
The Ghostly Rental. *Scribner's Monthly*, September.
Cousin et Cousine. *La Revue des deux Mondes*, October 1.
Daniel Deronda: a Conversation. *Atlantic Monthly*, December.

1877

Normandy and Pyrenees. *The Galaxy*, January.
Letters of Balzac. *The Galaxy*, February. Reprinted in *French Poets and Novelists* (1878).
The Théâtre Français. *The Galaxy*, April. Reprinted in *French Poets and Novelists* (1878).
Theatres of London. *The Galaxy*, May.
Alfred de Musset. *The Galaxy*, June. Reprinted in *French Poets and Novelists* (1878).
George Sand. *The Galaxy*, July. Reprinted in *French Poets and Novelists* (1878).
The Picture Season in London. *The Galaxy*, August.
Three Excursions. *The Galaxy*, September. Epsom; Hatfield House; Oxford at Commemoration. Reprinted in *Portraits of Places* (1883).
Four Meetings. *Scribner's Monthly*, November. Reprinted in *The Author of Beltraffio* (1884).
In Warwickshire. *The Galaxy*, November. Reprinted in *Portraits of Places* (1883), also *English Hours* (1905).
The Suburbs of London. *The Galaxy*, December.

The American. Boston: James R. Osgood & Co., 1877 (present publisher: Houghton, Mifflin & Co.).

1878

A Little Tour in France. *Atlantic Monthly*, January. Journey into sections east of Paris.
Italy Revisited. *Atlantic Monthly*, April.
Recent Florence. *Atlantic Monthly*, May.
Daisy Miller: A Study. *Cornhill Magazine*, June–July.
An International Episode. *Cornhill Magazine*. December–January, 1879.
The Europeans. *Atlantic Monthly*, July–October.
Langstaff's Marriage. *Scribner's Monthly*, August.
Quatre rencontres. *La Revue des deux Mondes*, December 15.
The Europeans: A Sketch. Boston: Houghton, Osgood & Co., 1878 (present publisher: Houghton, Mifflin & Co.); London: Macmillan & Co.
Watch and Ward. Boston: Houghton, Osgood & Co., 1878 (present publisher: Houghton, Mifflin & Co.).
French Poets and Novelists. London and New York: Macmillan & Co., 1878.

 Contains: Alfred de Musset (1877); Théophile Gautier (1873); Charles Baudelaire; Honoré de Balzac (1875); Balzac's Letters (1877); George Sand (1877); Charles de Bernard and Gustave Flaubert (1876); Ivan Turgénieff (1874); The Two Ampères (1875); Madame de Sabran (1875); Mérimée's Letters; The Théâtre Français (December, 1876).

 2d edition, 1884; reprinted (Globe 8vo.), 1893, 1904.

Daisy Miller: a Study. New York: Harper & Bros. (No. 82 of Harper's *Half-Hour Series*.) Reprinted in 1892 with illustrations by Harry McVickar.

An International Episode. New York: Harper & Bros. (No. 91 of *Harper's Half-Hour Series*.) Reprinted in 1892 with illustrations by Harry McVickar.

1879

The Pension Beaurepas. *Atlantic Monthly*, April. Reprinted in *The Siege of London* (1883).

A Friend of Lord Byron. *North American Review*, April. Review of Memoir of the Rev. Francis Hodgson, B.D.

Diary of a Man of Fifty. *Harper's Magazine*, July; also *Macmillan's Magazine*, July. Reprinted in *The Madonna of the Future* (1879).

The Madonna of the Future. London and New York: Macmillan & Co., 1879.

Contains also: A Bundle of Letters; The Diary of a Man of Fifty (1879); Eugene Pickering (1874).

Hawthorne. New York: Harper & Bros., 1879; London: Macmillan & Co. (Morley's *English Men of Letters*.)

Roderick Hudson. Boston: Houghton, Osgood & Co., 1879 (present publisher: Houghton, Mifflin & Co.).

Reverse of title-page contains following note: Roderick Hudson was originally published in Boston in 1875. It has now been minutely revised and has received a large number of verbal alterations. Several passages have been rewritten.

The Diary of a Man of Fifty and A Bundle of Letters. New York: Harper & Bros. (No. 135 of *Harper's Half-Hour Series*.)

1880

Sainte-Beuve. *North American Review*, January. Review of Correspondance de C. A. Sainte-Beuve.
Washington Square. *Harper's Magazine*, July–December. Published in book form in 1881.
Confidence. *Scribner's Monthly*, August–December, 1880; January 1881.
The Portrait of a Lady. *Atlantic Monthly*, November, 1880–December, 1881.
Confidence. Boston: Houghton, Osgood & Co., 1880 (present publisher: Houghton, Mifflin & Co.).

1881

The Portrait of a Lady. Boston: Houghton, Mifflin & Co., 1881; London: Macmillan & Co., 3 vols.
Washington Square. Illustrated by George du Maurier. New York: Harper & Bros., 1881.

1882

Alphonse Daudet. *Atlantic Monthly*, June.
Venice. *Century Magazine*, November.
The Point of View. *Century Magazine*, December. Reprinted in *The Siege of London* (1882).

1883

Tomasso Salvini. *Atlantic Monthly*, March.
Daisy Miller: a Comedy. *Atlantic Monthly*, April–June. Published in book form in 1883.

Du Maurier and London Society. *Century Magazine*, May. Reprinted in *Partial Portraits* (1888).
The Correspondence of Carlyle and Emerson. *Century Magazine*, June.
Anthony Trollope. *Century Magazine*, July. Reprinted in *Partial Portraits* (1888).
En Provence. *Atlantic Monthly*, July–November, 1883; February, April, May, 1884. Reprinted as A Little Tour in France (1884).
Alphonse Daudet. *Century Magazine*, August. Reprinted in *Partial Portraits* (1888).
The Impressions of a Cousin. *Century Magazine*, November–December. Reprinted in *Tales of Three Cities* (1883).
Daisy Miller: a Comedy. In three acts. Boston: James R. Osgood & Co. (present publisher: Houghton, Mifflin & Co.). 1883.
The Siege of London. Boston: Houghton, Mifflin & Co.; London: Macmillan & Co., 1883. James R. Osgood & Co. (present publisher: Houghton, Mifflin & Co.).
    Contains also: The Pension Beaurepas (1879); The Point of View (1882).
Portraits of Places. Boston: James R. Osgood & Co., 1883 (present publisher: Houghton, Mifflin & Co.); London: Macmillan & Co., 1883.
    Contains: Venice (1882); Italy Revisited (1877); Occasional Paris (1877); Reims and Laon; A Little Tour (1876); Chartres (1876); Rouen (1876); Étretat (1876); From Normandy to the Pyrenees (1876); An English Easter (1877); London at Midsummer (1877);

Two Excursions: Epsom and Oxford at Commemoration (1877); In Warwickshire (1877); Abbeys and Castles (1877); English Vignettes (1879); An English New Year (1879); An English Watering-Place (1879); Saratoga (1870); Newport (1870); Quebec (1871); Niagara (1871).

The foregoing dates mark the year in which articles were contributed either to *The Nation*, *The Atlantic Monthly*, or *The Galaxy*.

Daisy Miller, Four Meetings, Langstaff's Marriage. London: Macmillan & Co., 1883.

1884

Ivan Turgénieff. *Atlantic Monthly*, January. Reprinted in *Partial Portraits* (1888).

Lady Barbarina. *Century Magazine*, May–July.

A New England Winter. *Century Magazine*, August–September. Reprinted in *Tales of Three Cities* (1884).

The Art of Fiction. *Longmans' Magazine*, September. Reply to W. Besant's lecture on The Art of Fiction delivered at the Royal Institution, April 25, 1884. Reprinted in *Partial Portraits* (1888); also combined with Besant's Art of Fiction (Cupples & Ford, Boston, 1884); again in *The Writer*, September, 1899.

A Little Tour in France. Boston: James R. Osgood & Co. (present publisher: Houghton, Mifflin & Co.), 1884.

Through Touraine, Gascony, Provence, etc.

New edition, with illustrations by Joseph Pennell, in 1900.

Tales of Three Cities. Boston: James R. Osgood & Co., 1884 (present publisher: Houghton, Mifflin & Co.).

Contains: The Impressions of a Cousin (1883) — a tale of New York; Lady Barbarina (1884) —a tale of London and New York; A New England Winter (1884)—a tale of Boston.

1885

George Eliot's Life. *Atlantic Monthly*, May.
The Bostonians. *Century Magazine*, February, 1885–February, 1886.
The Princess Casamassima. *Atlantic Monthly*, September, 1885 – October, 1886. Published in book form in 1886.
The Author of Beltraffio. Boston: James R. Osgood & Co., 1885 (present publisher: Houghton, Mifflin & Co.).

Contains also: Pandora; Georgina's Reasons; The Path of Duty; Four Meetings (1877).
Stories Revived. First and Second Series. 2 vols.; also 3 vols. London: Macmillan & Co., 1885.

Contents: Vol. I.—The Author of Beltraffio; Pandora; The Path of Duty; A Day of Days (1866). Vol. II.—A Light Man (1869); Georgina's Reason; A Passionate Pilgrim (1871); Rose-Agathe (1878). Vol. III.—Poor Richard (1867); The Last of the Valerii (1874); Master Eustace (1871); The Romance of Certain Old Clothes (1868); A Most Extraordinary Case (1868).

Not issued in America.

1886

William Dean Howells. *Harper's Weekly*, June 19.

Edwin A. Abbey. *Harper's Weekly*, December 4. Reprinted in *Picture and Text* (1893).

The Bostonians. New York: Macmillan & Co., 1 vol.; London: Macmillan & Co., 3 vols., 1886.

The Princess Casamassima. New York: Macmillan & Co., 1 vol.; London: Macmillan & Co., 3 vols., 1886.

1887

Coquelin. *Century Magazine*, January.

Constance Fenimore Woolson. *Harper's Weekly*, February 12. Reprinted in *Partial Portraits* (1888).

John S. Sargent. *Harper's Magazine*, October. Reprinted in *Picture and Text* (1893).

Cousin Maria. *Harper's Weekly*, August 6, 13, 20. Illustrated by C. S. Reinhart.

Emerson. *Macmillan's Magazine*, December.

1888

Louisa Pallant. *Harper's Magazine*, February. Illustrated by C. S. Reinhart. Reprinted in *The Aspern Papers* (1888).

Guy de Maupassant. *Fortnightly Review*, March. Reprinted in *Partial Portraits* (1888).

The Aspern Papers. *Atlantic Monthly*, March–May. Published in book form in 1888.

Robert Louis Stevenson. *Century Magazine*, April. Reprinted in *Partial Portraits* (1888).

The Liar. *Century Magazine*, May. Reprinted in *A London Life* (1889).

Two Countries. *Harper's Magazine*, June. Reprinted as The Modern Warning in *The Aspern Papers* (1888).
A London Life. *Scribner's Magazine*, June–September. Published in book form in 1889.
London. *Century Magazine*, December. Illustrations by Joseph Pennell. Reprinted in *Essays in London and Elsewhere* (1893).
The Aspern Papers, Louisa Pallant, The Modern Warning. London and New York: Macmillan & Co., 1888. 2 vols., also 1 vol.
Partial Portraits. London: Macmillan & Co., 1888. Reprinted 1894, 1899.

    Contains: Emerson (1887); The Life of George Eliot (1885); Daniel Deronda: a Conversation (1876); Anthony Trollope (1883); Robert Louis Stevenson (1887); Miss Woolson (1887); Alphonse Daudet (1883); Guy de Maupassant (1888); Ivan Turgénieff (1884); George du Maurier (1883); The Art of Fiction (1884).
The Reverberator. London and New York: Macmillan & Co., 1888.

1889

The Tragic Muse. *Atlantic Monthly*, January, 1889–May, 1890. Published in book form in 1890.
After the Play. *New Review*, June. Reprinted in *Picture and Text* (1893).
An Animated Conversation. *Scribner's Magazine*, March. Reprinted in *Essays in London and Elsewhere* (1893).
Our Artists in Europe. *Harper's Magazine*, June. Reprinted under other titles in *Picture and Text* (1893).

Guy de Maupassant. *Harper's Weekly*, October 19.

The Solution. *New Review*, December, 1889–February, 1890. Reprinted in *The Lesson of the Master* (1892).

A London Life, The Patagonia, The Liar, Mrs. Temperly. London and New York: Macmillan & Co., 1889.

The Odd Number. Thirteen Tales. By Guy de Maupassant. The Translation by Jonathan Sturges. An Introduction by Henry James. New York: Harper & Bros., 1889.

1890

Daumier, Caricaturist. *Century Magazine* January. With illustrations. Reprinted in *Picture and Text* (1893).

Charles S. Reinhart. *Harper's Weekly*, June 14. Reprinted in *Picture and Text* (1893).

Port Tarascon: the Last Adventures of the Illustrious Tartarin. Translated by Henry James. With preface by the translator. New York: Harper & Bros., 1890.

The Tragic Muse. Boston: Houghton, Mifflin & Co., 2 vols., 1890; London: Macmillan & Co., 3 vols., 1890.

1891

The Science of Criticism. *New Review*, May.

Brooksmith. *Harper's Weekly*, May 2. Reprinted in *The Lesson of the Master* (1891).

On the Occasion of Hedda Gabler. *New Review*, June. Reprinted in *Essays in London and Elsewhere* (1893).

The Marriages. *Atlantic Monthly*, August. Reprinted in *The Lesson of the Master* (1891).
The Chaperon. *Atlantic Monthly*, November–December. Reprinted in *The Real Thing* (1893).

1892

James Russell Lowell. *Atlantic Monthly*, January. Reprinted in *Essays in London and Elsewhere* (1893).
Mrs. Humphry Ward. *English Illustrated Magazine*, February. Reprinted in *Essays in London and Elsewhere* (1893).
Nona Vincent. *English Illustrated Magazine*, February–March. Illustrations by W. J. Hennessy. Reprinted in *The Real Thing* (1893).
The Private Life. *Atlantic Monthly*, April. Published in book form in 1893.
Lord Beauprey. *Macmillan's Magazine*, April–June. Reprinted in *The Private Life* (1893).
Wolcott Balestier. *Cosmopolitan Magazine*, May.
Jersey Villas. *Cosmopolitan Magazine*, July–August. Illustrated by Irving R. Wiles. Reprinted as Sir Dominick Farrand in *The Real Thing* (1893).
Collaboration. *English Illustrated Magazine*, September. Reprinted in *The Wheel of Time* (1893).
The Grand Canal. *Scribner's Magazine*, November. Illustrations by Alexander Zezzos. Reprinted in *The Great Streets of the World*. New York: Charles Scribner's Sons, 1892.
The Wheel of Time. *Cosmopolitan Magazine*, December, 1892–January, 1893. Published in book form in 1893.

Daisy Miller and An International Episode. Illustrated from drawings by Harry W. McVickar. New York: Harper & Bros., 1892.
The Average Woman. By Wolcott Balestier. Preface by Henry James. American Publishing Corporation, 1892; United States Book Co.
The Lesson of the Master. London and New York: Macmillan & Co., 1892.

 Contains also: The Marriages (1891); The Pupil; Brooksmith (1891); Sir Edmund Orme.

1893

Gustave Flaubert. *Macmillan's Magazine*, March. Reprinted in *Essays in London and Elsewhere* (1893).
Frances Anne Kemble. *Temple Bar*, April. Reprinted in *Essays in London and Elsewhere* (1893).
The Middle Years. *Scribner's Magazine*, May. Reprinted in *Terminations* (1895).
Essays in London and Elsewhere. New York: Harper & Bros., 1893; London: James R. Osgood; McIlvaine & Co., 1893.

 Contains: London (1888); James Russell Lowell (1891); Frances Anne Kemble (1893); Gustave Flaubert (1893); Pierre Loti (1888); Journal of the Brothers de Goncourt (1888); Browning in Westminster Abbey (1890); Henrik Ibsen; On the Occasion of Hedda Gabler; On the Occasion of The Master Builder (1891–1893); Mrs. Humphry Ward (1891); Criticism (1891); An Animated Conversation (1889).

Picture and Text. New York: Harper & Bros.
  Contains: Black and White (1889); Edwin A. Abbey; Charles S. Reinhart; Alfred Parsons; John S. Sargent (1887); Honoré Daumier (1890); After the Play (1889).

The Private Life. London: James R. Osgood; McIlvaine & Co., 1893.
  Contains also: The Wheel of Time (1892); Lord Beaupré (1892); The Visits; Collaboration (1892); Owen Wingrave.

The Private Life, The Visits, Lord Beaupré. New York: Harper & Bros., 1893.

The Wheel of Time, Collaboration, Owen Wingrave. New York: Harper & Bros., 1893.

The Real Thing and Other Tales.. New York and London: Macmillan & Co., 1893.
  Contains also: Sir Dominick Farrand (1892); Nona Vincent (1892); The Chaperon (1891); Greville Fane.

1894

George du Maurier. *Harper's Weekly*, April 14.

The Death of the Lion. *The Yellow Book*, London, April. Reprinted in *Terminations* (1895).

The Coxon Fund. *The Yellow Book*, London, July. Reprinted in *Terminations* (1895).
  This volume of *The Yellow Book* also contains a portrait sketch of the author by Sargent.

Theatricals. Two Comedies: Tenants, Disengaged. London: James R. Osgood; McIlvaine & Co., 1894; New York: Harper & Bros., 1894.

Theatricals. Second Series: The Album, The Reprobate. London: James R. Osgood; McIlvaine & Co.; New York: Harper & Bros., 1894.

1895

The Next Time. *The Yellow Book*, London, July. Reprinted in *Embarrassments* (1896).

Guy Domville. Mr. Henry James' Guy Domville: An Appreciation, by A. B. Walkley. *Harper's Weekly*, March 2.

    This drama was produced in London at the St. James Theatre, January 5, but has never been printed. The foregoing article contains an analysis of the play and a few citations.

Terminations: The Death of the Lion, The Coxon Fund, The Middle Years, The Altar of the Dead. New York: Harper & Bros., 1895.

1896

The Figure in the Carpet. *Cosmopolis*, January. Simultaneously in *The Chap Book*, Chicago. Reprinted in *Embarrassments* (1896).

Glasses. *Atlantic Monthly*, February. Reprinted in *Embarrassments* (1896).

On the Death of Alexander Dumas the Younger (November 27, 1895). *New Review*, March.

The Old Things. *Atlantic Monthly*, April–October. Published in book form as The Spoils of Poynton (1897).

The Way It Came. *The Chap Book*, May 1. Reprinted in *Embarrassments* (1896).

Mr. Henry Irving's Production of Cymbeline. *Harper's Weekly*, November 21.

Embarrassments. London and New York: Macmillan & Co., 1896.

    Contains: The Figure in the Carpet (1896); Glasses (1896); The Next Time (1895); The Way It Came (1896).

The Other House. New York: The Macmillan Co.; London: Macmillan & Co., Ltd., 1896. Issued October, 1896; reprinted, November, 1896.

1897

He and She: Recent Documents. *The Yellow Book*, London, January.
    On the intimacy of George Sand and Alfred de Musset.

What Maisie Knew. *New Review*, February–July. Simultaneously in *The Chap Book*, Chicago, January 15–August 1. Published in book form in 1897.

George du Maurier. *Harper's Magazine*, September.

What Maisie Knew. London: Heinemann & Co.; Chicago: Herbert S. Stone & Co., 1897.

London Letters in *Harper's Weekly*.
    Dated January 1. Irving's Richard III.; Jane Robins in Ibsen; Watts's pictures. Published January 23.
    January 15. Ibsen's John Gabriel Borkman. Published February 6.
    February 1. Marks's Life and Letters of Frederick Walker; Pictures at Burlington House and Grafton Gallery. Published February 20.
    March 3. Forty-one Years in India (Lord Roberts); Hunter's The Thackerays in India; Steel, On the Face of the Waters. Published March 27.
    April 3. Mr. Archer on the Drama; Forbes-Robertson; Mrs. Patrick Campbell; Beerbohm

Tree; Charles Wyndham. Published April 24,
May 5. The Spring Exhibitions—Abbey.
Sargent. Published June 5.
June 1. Queen's Jubilee. Published June 26.
July 1. George Gissing. Published July 31.
July 31. Paul Bouget at Oxford; Mrs. Oliphant. Published August 21.
August 31. Old Suffolk. Published September 25. Reprinted in *English Hours* (1905).
October 16. English Politics. Published November 6.
The Spoils of Poynton. Boston and New York: Houghton, Mifflin & Co., 1897; London, Heinemann & Co., 1897.
Last Studies of Hubert Crackenthorpe. With an Introduction by Henry James. London: Heinemann & Co., November, 1897.

1898

John Delavoy. *Cosmopolis*, January–February. Reprinted in *The Soft Side* (1900).
The Late James Payn. *Illustrated London News*, April 9.
The Story-teller at Large: Mr. Henry Harland. *Fortnightly Review*, April.
Prosper Mérimée. *Literature*, July 23.
The Awkward Age. *Harper's Weekly*, October 1, 1898–January 7, 1899. Published in book form in 1899.
American Letter. *Literature*, vol. ii.
March 26. Question of Opportunities.
April 9. The International and the Local; Henry Harland; American Wives and English Husbands (Mrs. Atherton).

Bibliography

 April 16. General Grant's Letters; Walt Whitman; Richard Harding Davis.
 April 23. American Ideals (Roosevelt); Essays on the Civil War and Reconstruction (Dunning); The Workers (Wyckoff).
 April 30. The Celebrity (Churchill); Soldier of Manhattan (Altsheler); The General's Double (Captain King).
 June 11. American Magazines; Across the Everglades (Willoughby); Cheerful Yesterdays (Higginson); Emerson and Other Essays (Chapman).
 June 25. Unforeseen Tendencies in Democracy (Godkin); Meaning of Education (Butler).
 July 9. The Novel of Dialect; The Durket Sperret (Barnwell-Elliott); The Juggler (Craddock); The Preference for the Study of the Primitive; The Story of a Play (Howells); Silence (Wilkins).

Alphonse Daudet. *Literature*, December 25.
In the Cage. Chicago and New York: Herbert S. Stone & Co., 1898; London: Duckworth, August, 1898.
The Two Magics: The Turn of the Screw, Covering End. New York: The Macmillan Co., 1898; London: Duckworth, August, 1898. American edition set up and electrotyped, September 18, 1898. Reprinted October, 1898; January, April, May, 1899; March, 1905.
Pierre Loti's Impressions. Introduction by Henry James. London: Constable, November, 1898.
Nathaniel Hawthorne. *Warner Library of the World's Best Literature.*

James Russell Lowell. *Warner Library of the World's Best Literature.*
Ivan Turgénieff. *Warner Library of the World's Best Literature.*

1899

Europe. *Scribner's Magazine*, June. Reprinted in *The Soft Side* (1900).
Present Literary Situation in France. *North American Review*, October.
The Awkward Age. New York: Harper & Bros., 1899; London: Heinemann & Co., April, 1899.

1900

Letters of Robert Louis Stevenson. *North American Review*, January.
The Great Good Place. *Scribner's Magazine*, January. Reprinted in *The Soft Side* (1900).
Maud-Evelyn. *Atlantic Monthly*, April. Reprinted in *The Soft Side* (1900).
Miss Gunton of Poughkeepsie. *Cornhill Magazine*, May. Reprinted in *The Soft Side* (1900).
The Tone of Time. *Scribner's Magazine*, November. Reprinted in *The Better Sort* (1903).
Broken Wings. *Century Magazine*, December. Reprinted in *The Better Sort* (1903).
The Vicar of Wakefield. A Tale. By Oliver Goldsmith. With an Introduction by Henry James. New York: The Century Co., 1900.
The Soft Side. New York: The Macmillan Co., 1900; London: Methuen & Co., 8vo., September, 1900.

    Contains: The Great Good Place (1900); Europe (1899); Paste; The Real Right Thing;

The Great Condition; The Tree of Knowledge; The Abasement of the Northmores; The Given Case; John Delavoy (1898); The Third Person; Maud-Evelyn (1900); Miss Gunton of Poughkeepsie (1900).

A Little Tour in France. With illustrations by Joseph Pennell. Boston and New York: Houghton, Mifflin & Co., 1900. First English edition—London: Heinemann & Co., 8vo, pp. 350. Published October, 1900. New preface signed London, August 6, 1899.

1901

Winchelsea, Rye, and "Denis Duval." *Scribner's Magazine*, January. Pictures by E. Peixotto. Reprinted in *English Hours* (1905).

Matilde Serao. *North American Review*, March.

The Two Faces. *Cornhill Magazine*, June. Reprinted in *The Better Sort* (1903).

The Beldonald Holbein. *Harper's Magazine*, October. Illustrations by Lucius Hitchcock. Reprinted in *The Better Sort* (1903).

Edmund Rostand. *Cornhill Magazine*, November; *The Critic*, November.

Faces. *Harper's Bazaar*, December.

The Sacred Fount. New York: Charles Scribner's Sons, 1901; London: Methuen & Co., February, 1901.

1902

The Late Mrs. Arthur Bronson. *The Critic*, February.

George Sand: The New Life. *North American Review*, April.

Flickerbridge. *Scribner's Magazine*, February. Reprinted in *The Better Sort* (1903).

The Wings of the Dove. 2 vols. New York: Charles Scribner's Sons, 1902 (published August); London: Constable, cr. 8vo. (published September, 1902).

Flaubert's Madame Bovary. With critical introduction by Henry James. 8vo, pp. 486. Heinemann, May, 1902.

Balzac's Two Young Brides. With critical introduction by Henry James. 8vo, pp. 417. Heinemann, September, 1902.

The two foregoing included in Heinemann's *Century of French Romance*.

1903

The Ambassadors. *North American Review*, January–December. Published in book form in 1903.

Émile Zola. *Atlantic Monthly*, August.

The Better Sort. New York: Charles Scribner's Sons, 1903; London: Methuen & Co., 8vo, February, 1903.

Contains: Broken Wings (1900); The Beldonald Holbein (1901); The Two Faces (1901); The Tone of Time (1900); The Special Type; Mrs. Medwin; Flickerbridge (1902); The Story in It; The Beast in the Jungle; The Birthplace; The Papers.

The Ambassadors. New York: Harper & Bros. (published November, 1903); London: Methuen & Co., 8vo (published September, 1903).

William Wetmore Story and His Friends. From Letters, Diaries, and Recollections. In two volumes. Boston: Houghton, Mifflin & Co., 1903; London: William Blackwood & Sons, 2 vols., 8vo, October, 1903.

1904

Gabrielle d'Annunzio. *Quarterly Review*, April.
Fordham Castle. *Harper's Magazine*, December.
The Golden Bowl. 2 vols. New York: Charles Scribner's Sons, 1904 (published November).

1905

New England: An Autumn Impression. *North American Review*, April–June.
The Lesson of Balzac. *Atlantic Monthly*, August.
The Question of Our Speech. *Appleton's Booklover's Magazine*, August.
The Question of Our Speech.
    Containing also The Lesson of Balzac. Two lectures. By Henry James. Boston and New York: Houghton, Mifflin & Co., 1905. 300 copies of the first edition bound uncut.
English Hours. By Henry James. With illustrations by Joseph Pennell. Boston and New York: Houghton, Mifflin & Co., 1905.
    Contains: London; Browning in Westminster Abbey; Chester; Litchfield and Warwick; North Devon; Wells and Salisbury; An English Easter; London at Midsummer; Two Excursions; In Warwickshire; Abbeys and Castles; English Vignettes; An English New Year; An English Watering-place; Winchelsea, Rye, and "Denis Duval"; Old Suffolk.